ANIMATION
HOW-TO
CD

Jeff Bowermaster

Waite
Group
Press™

Corte Madera, California

Publisher: *Mitchell Waite*
Editorial Director: *Scott Calamar*
Managing Editor: *John Crudo*
Content Editor: *Harry Henderson*
Technical Reviewer: *David K. Mason*
Design and Production: *Michele Cuneo*
Illustrations: *Pat Rogondino*
Production Director: *Julianne Ososke*

Printed in the United States of America
94 95 96 97 • 10 9 8 7 6 5 4 3 2 1

Library of Congress Cataloging in Publication Data
Bowermaster, Jeff.
   Animation how-to CD / Jeff Bowermaster.
      p.   cm.
   Includes index.
   ISBN: 1-878739-54-9: $39.95
   1. Computer animation. I. Title.
TR897.5.B69   1994
006.6'765--dc20
                                                        93-43050
                                                            CIP

DEDICATION

o David McCurry, for keeping the wetware stoked while I phased.

ACKNOWLEDGMENTS

The bulk of the credit for the contents goes to the crowd at the YCCMR and TGA BBSs for giving me my education. At the risk of leaving out some important people, here goes: John Hammerton, Dan Farmer, Truman Brown, Mike Miller, Steve Anger, Adam Shiffman, Derek Taylor, Ken Koehler, Doug Reedy, Heinz Schuller, Karl Weller, Chris Smotherman, Douglas Otwell, Jay Sprenkle, John Calcagno, and Jay Schumacher. Their incredible enthusiasm, generosity, and openness provided a nonstop source of inspiration.

Alexander Enzmann and David Mason deserve a round of applause for providing a great ray tracer and a flic builder that are easy, powerful, and for the most part, bug-free. Special thanks go to Eric Deren for being clever, talented, creative, and skilled at uttering the phrase "How's the book coming?"

I'd also sincerely like to thank the folks at Waite Group Press (Mitch Waite, John Crudo, and Michele Cuneo) and the technical talents of Harry Henderson and David Mason for their recommendations and technical expertise.

ABOUT THE AUTHOR

Jeff Bowermaster got hooked on computer graphics in June 1991 after reading about the DKB ray tracer in *Byte Magazine* and connecting with the folks at the You Can Call Me Ray BBS. He has been animating ray traced images ever since, and has collected a small pile of PCs that double in speed and quadruple in hard disk space each year. He spent eight years racing bicycles and now tortures himself training with those who still do, and lifting weights to make him too heavy to hang on. He has a Ph.D. in Chemistry and works for an agricultural chemical company.

Dear Reader/Viewer:

What is a book? Is it perpetually fated to be inky words on a paper page? Or can a book simply be something that inspires—feeding your head with ideas and creativity regardless of the medium? The latter, I believe. That's why I'm always pushing our books to a higher plane; using new technology to reinvent the medium.

I wrote my first book in 1973, *Projects in Sights, Sounds, and Sensations.* I like to think of it as our first multimedia book. In the years since then, I've learned that people want to *experience* information, not just passively absorb it—they want interactive MTV in a book. With this in mind, I started my own publishing company and published *Master C,* a book/disk package that turned the PC into a C language instructor. Then we branched out to computer graphics with *Fractal Creations,* which included a color poster, 3-D glasses, and a totally rad fractal generator. Ever since, we've included disks and other goodies with most of our books. *Virtual Reality Creations* is bundled with 3-D Fresnel viewing goggles and *Walkthroughs and Flybys CD* comes with a multimedia CD-ROM. We've made complex multimedia accessible for any PC user with *Ray Tracing Creations, Multimedia Creations, Making Movies on Your PC, Image Lab,* and three books on Fractals.

The Waite Group continues to publish innovative multimedia books on cutting-edge topics, and of course the programming books that make up our heritage. Being a programmer myself, I appreciate clear guidance through a tricky OS, so our books come bundled with disks and CDs loaded with code, utilities and custom controls.

By 1993, The Waite Group published 135 books. Our next step is to develop a new type of book, an interactive, multimedia experience involving the reader on many levels.

With this new book, you'll be trained by a computer-based instructor with infinite patience, run a simulation to visualize the topic, play a game that shows you different aspects of the subject, interact with others on-line, and have instant access to a large database on the subject. For traditionalists, there will be a full-color, paper-based book.

In the meantime, they've wired the White House for hi-tech; the information super highway has been proposed; and computers, communication, entertainment, and information are becoming inseparable. To travel in this Digital Age you'll need guidebooks. The Waite Group offers such guidance for the most important software— your mind.

We hope you enjoy this book. For a color catalog, just fill out and send in the Reader Report Card at the back of the book. You can reach me on CIS as 75146,3515, MCI mail as mwaite, and usenet as mitch@well.sf.ca.us.

Mitchell Waite

Mitchell Waite
Publisher

Waite
Group
Press™

TABLE OF CONTENTS

Contents

INTRODUCTION

With computer animation using ray traced graphics, you can create *anything*. Flocks of transparent, skydiving vampire frogs, colliding planets with boiling yellow oceans, elastic spiraling waterfalls, marching columns of pencils with outrageous splurting erasers... anything you can think of, you can create. It's a never ending journey of discovery. It's not like mastering all the commands in some software package and then applying them systematically to solve problems like balancing your checkbook—you get to make all this stuff up as you go along. You wander off into a world of your own creation and decide how you'd like reality to function there. You make up your own rules, create your own tools, set up your own systems and generate whatever you like. You'll no doubt borrow heavily from your experience in this world, but you're not limited by any of its restrictions.

This book describes in detail the process used to generate over 50 ray traced animations. With variations, there are actually over 200 flics, and all the animations are included on the CD-ROM. For a quick preview (and a data rush), a script file has been included to allow you to view all of them at once as soon as you break the seal.

Is This Book For You?

This book chronicles journeys into these other worlds. Its intended audience is people who have some familiarity with computer graphics in addition to basic programming skills. For these people, this book explains powerful procedures and ways of achieving some truly stunning animations and effects.

If you're new to this type of graphics, don't worry. Everything you need to get started is included here. You can pick up the necessary skills by rendering the examples, and reading the code. You can generate some wonderful animations during the learning phase by experimenting to see what certain variables do when given a sequence of different values. Although many people are put off by ray tracing syntax, it's really not that hard to master. It doesn't hurt (much), it sinks in fairly fast, and I'm sure those of you who've already gone through it will agree it's pretty amazing when the bulb clicks on and you realize, "I'm in charge here!"

Where's the GUI?

What might seem strange to many people is that ray tracers (Vivid, Polyray, POV-Ray and Rayshade) are graphics programs without graphical interfaces. It's all text. Scene creation is done by an iterative process of editing, rendering, frowning, and repeating the cycle until a grin is achieved. Motion is added programmatically.

This apparent liability actually turns out to be an asset for most people who stick with it. It forces them to think of scenes mathematically in terms of viewpoints, objects, and lights (see Figure I-1). It's precise, it's controlled, and best of all, it can be automated. Then animation becomes just a matter of herding objects, textures, or indeed any scene descriptor programmatically to create orchestrated effects that would be difficult or at least incredibly tedious to do manually.

This book focuses on making scenes move using programs and functions. You should realize that while 3D Studio, Topas, and other high end PC design tools are terrific (if you can afford them), a basic understanding of ray tracing and the principles of scene construction make it possible to create really great scenes without having to spend a dime on the interface. It all comes down to the amount of time you can devote to learning the graphics, versus the amount of convenience you can afford. In a commercial setting, something like 3D Studio can save a great deal of time and effort, but the fundamental effects you create boil down to careful thought and planning, regardless of the tools you use.

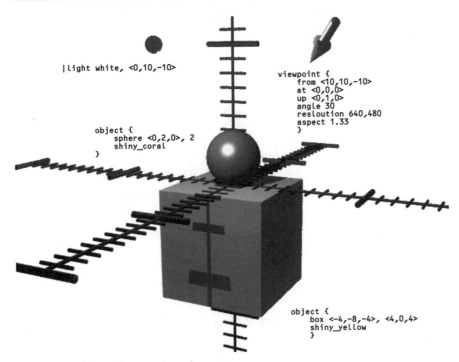

Figure I-1 Mathematical representation of a scene

Format

This is a hands-on, code-intensive book. The code always preceeds its explanation, but don't let that throw you. Every new concept is covered in detail in the text that follows the code.

Eight chapters contain sample animations that highlight unique effects or principles. An individual animation begins with a description, followed in most cases by a simulation that selects the appropriate values for the control variables. The simulation forms the basis for data files that the ray tracer uses to create the final series of images. Each step in the process is explained in sufficient detail to allow you to employ the principles involved and create animations of your own.

Don't panic. There's no major calculus or cryptic syntax to throw you. No brain cells were harmed in the creation of this code. But this book is by no means what could be described as "content-free." Covered are many useful items such as splines, functions, particle systems, bizarre textures, and motions, with each section focusing in on one particular aspect in the animation process. You'll get the opportunity to play with specific types of animation, and later on combine those principles to make more complex creations. Using the code that was used to create the sample aminations, you'll be able to combine whatever effects you like to create whatever you want.

What You Need

This book and CD, when combined with the proper computer and operating system, provide the resources you need to produce high-end animations.

The Tools Included on the Disc

The Polyray Ray Tracer is the primary rendering engine. It uses simple text files to generate photorealistic images. A series of these images linked together make up your animation. Dave's TGA Animator (DTA) is used to convert a series of images into an animation file called a flic, and can also convert 24-bit targa files, which can't be displayed well by standard VGA adapters, into 8-bit GIF files, which can. The animation player AAPLAYHI is also included for viewing these flics and GIFs.

The Tools You'll Need to Have Yourself

You'll need a decent text editor and Microsoft QuickBasic (which is packaged with MS-DOS 5.0 and above). QuickBasic is used to write simple visualizers, to automate the more tedious aspects of orchestrating complex motions, and to deal with things like several hundred objects at once. Fortunately, QBASIC and EDIT are included with DOS 5.0 (and above).

It wouldn't hurt if you had access to the full QuickBasic package. Editors, like keyboards and word processors, are a matter of personal preference; feel free to use whatever you're comfortable with, but note that an editor with a macro programming language (such as BRIEF or QEDIT) can reduce your work enormously.

Hardware Requirements

Let's not beat around the bush here; ray tracing consumes more raw horsepower than most planet-wide terraforming operations, and carbon-based life forms have annoyingly short life (not to mention attention) spans. Ray tracing is the perfect application to justify getting the newest, fastest, most powerful computer you can find.

The *minimum* system required is a 386 DX with a 387 coprocessor, but a 486 DX or DX2 would be even better. The three-to-one speed advantage of a 486 can be offset by running smaller images on a 386, so you'll still be able to make and display the animations in this book; they'll just either be smaller or take longer to create.

Don't even consider doing this on an SX or a 386 without a coprocessor. Coprocessors are cheap these days and can speed up image rendering 20 times or more. A 486/33 DX with 4MB, an SVGA, a 200MB hard drive, a mouse, and DOS 5.0 or above will get you by quite nicely. The present work was done on three 486s running around the clock for seven months. Memory is usually not a major consideration, and 4MBs is usually fine. It only becomes an issue when you're doing incredibly detailed heightfields or recursive objects. Note, however, that if you have sufficient memory to completely hold your flics in RAM, they play much more smoothly, because the disk transfer bottleneck is removed.

Hardware Wish List

Several items aren't exactly mandatory, but will probably make your life much easier (of course until the bills arrive). You might consider adding them to your wish list for the future or maxing out your credit, depending on your level of self-control.

Hard Drive

A larger hard drive makes dealing with longer animations easier. Flics tend to be huge, but the individual targa files they're built from can be enormous. It's usually a balancing act between blowing away something important ("Do I really need this DOS directory?") and having your animation run out of space sometime around 3 AM.

Tape Backup

A tape backup unit or other removable data storage medium comes in handy to preserve a record of your advancing prowess in computer graphics. QIC-80 tape units are available from several manufacturers, and the ones rated at

250 meg (a specification for compressed text files) will actually store 170-180 meg of flic files on media that goes for under $20.

24-bit Video Card

The first shocker about VGAs is they aren't perfect. The standard VGA 8-bit mode is a really terrible way to view the wonderful 24-bit images that Polyray generates. Some of you probably have hicolor VGAs or even Windows compatible 24-bit graphics accelerator cards. Using Windows graphics programs like Photoshop, Picture Publisher, Corel Paint, or indeed any Windows image editing program, is highly recommended to show off the true beauty of your images. Be aware that some of the older shareware graphics display programs floating around BBSs might not work well with them.

NTSC Video Output Card

A VGA to NTSC adapter will let you make video tapes and impress your friends. The standard inexpensive ones are not exactly broadcast quality, because there are differences between the aspect ratios and color tolerances of VGA and NTSC displays. But the thrill of seeing your work run to tape is blind to such minor flaws. Just don't expect "mind's eye" quality images.

The Tools

The tools supplied with and required by this book are relatively easy to use; however, you may not be familiar with some of the utilities. Essential information about installing and running these tools is provided here, but it's impossible (in my allotted space) to cover every aspect of their operation. The following introductions into QuickBasic, Polyray, DTA, and AAPLAYHI will get you started, and you'll learn much more about QuickBasic and Polyray as you go through the book's examples, because the code is the heart of the information.

In the allotted space, it's impossible to cover every aspect of QuickBasic use. The following introductions into QuickBasic, Polyray, DTA and AAPLAYHI cover what you'll need to know to get started. You'll end up learning much more about both QuickBasic and Polyray as you go through the examples in each chapter, because the code in this book is where all the real information lies.

The good thing about all this is that the codes are already written and tested, so sit back, relax, maybe grab some popcorn, and enjoy the ride.

Installing the Software

Before we begin to describe the tools, the software provided on the CD-ROM must be installed on your hard drive. Run the installation program, following the directions provided in this book. This will load the programs and utilities into the appropriate directories, ready for use. To find out how to install the provided tools, check out the Installation Guide.

Directories and Drives

Since you may choose to place these files on any drive letter you want, the issue of directory locations for specific files rears its ugly head. Every file in this book assumes you're running Polyray and your data files from the same drive, and demands that these files be contained in directories of a specific name. Provided you're comfortable dealing with directories, you can go in and establish any structure you like.

QuickBasic

Almost every animation created in this book is done with the assistance of QuickBasic. It's great for generating simulations and plotting mathematical functions. It's not particularly powerful or as portable as a language like C, but for what we're using it for, it doesn't have to be. It's easy to write code that runs right the first time.

Loading and Running

Even if you're new to QuickBasic, you'll be able to pick up what's being done here fairly fast. More information on the QBASIC IDE (Intergrated Development Environment) can be found in Appendix A, as well as the DOS documentation. The programs have already been written for you; running them is as simple as typing QBASIC (distributed with DOS) or QB, loading a .BAS file and running it. You may choose to use a mouse to move through the menus, or use the short cut commands to accomplish these actions.

Polyray

The CD contains an installation program that will automatically load the Polyray program, the data files, and all the utilities required into their proper locations.

The shareware version of Polyray includes a batch file that will create all the sample images supplied with Polyray. We didn't do that with the animations in this book because it would take a long time, and require several gigabytes of disk storage space. TGA files tend to form sprawling mounds, and it's useful, at least from a directory listing standpoint, to herd them together into their own subdirectories, use them to create flics, then blow them away.

Running Polyray

Detailed instructions are found in the Polyray documentation which cover all the intricacies of running Polyray and an overview can be found in Appendix A.

DTA

Polyray generates a series of TGA images in a numbered list. DTA assembles them in an animation.

You hand DTA the file prefix for the images, inform it that you want a flic, give it an output name, and a playing speed.

There are many switches in DTA, and please read Appendix A and the program documentation for more information. They're all very useful, but two in particular are used all the time. If you generate images for your flics that are larger than 320 x 200, you must use the /R6 switch to make a high resolution .FLC from them. There are other modes, so again, read the documentation. A quick summary is also available if you just enter the command DTA by itself with no other parameters.

One of the first tasks DTA must perform is generating an optimal palette to map the 16.7 million possible colors in the targa files into the best 256 colors to run on a standard VGA or SVGA display. This can be a lengthy process for animations that are several hundred frames long, and if the basic image doesn't change all that much, checking every single targa file doesn't really make higher quality images. You can scan, say, every 10th image using the /c10 switch, and this can really cut down the time it takes to make the final flic.

DTA generates GIFs using the /fg switch. As mentioned earlier, the animation player AAPLAYHI can then display these GIFs for you, although VPIC or CSHOW, two popular shareware GIF viewers, are more commonlly used for this task.

AAPLAYHI

AAPLAYHI is a freely distributable animation player program from Autodesk. The default maximum display size is 320 x 200, but with the appropriate video cards and VESA compatible modes, animations as large as

1,024 x 768 can be displayed. It not only works with flics, but will also display GIFs as well.

An AA.CFG file is created every time AAPLAYHI is started from a directory that doesn't contain one, and the screen size may be selected from whatever screen modes AAPLAYHI detects your hardware is capable of.

If your flic is 320 x 200 or smaller, you can run AAPLAYHI directly by entering the command AAPLAYHI flic.FLI. Entering AAPLAYHI by itself brings up a graphics screen and identifies the program. You press a mouse key to get to the menus. At this point, you'll either be able to load your flics directly or set the screen size to the appropriate one and load your flics afterwords.

AAPLAYHI will use all your system memory and attempt to load the flic into it, which makes flics play much smoother than directly off your hard drive. While it doesn't mind HIMEM, you cannot have EMM386 providing expanded memory or AAPLAYHI will key on it and miss your extended memory entirely.

Additional References

For additional information on the tools in this book, the following resources are available:

- Appendix A, Tools Reference covers QuickBasic, Polyray, DTA, and AAPLATYHI in greater depth.

- The complete documentation for Polyray and DTA on the CD, and your DOS manuals for more information about QuickBasic.

- If you're stumped and need extra help, the companion book *Making Movies on Your PC* would be a worthwhile resource for you. It provides a complete tutorial on Polyray and DTA by the authors of both programs, and introduces many of the concepts and techniques that we'll be using in this book.

- See installation for more information about loading the tools and code included on the CD.

Program Note

We have used the ⇐ character in this book to indicate program lines that "overflow" onto more than one line. The overflow character means that you should continue to type that line on one line. Do not type the ⇐ symbol or a carriage return.

The READ.ME File

Animation How-to CD includes over 450MB of resources, including the final animations, their source code, and the programs described in this book. On the root directory of the CD, you'll find a READ.ME file that explains how the resources are organized, how to use DOS commands to copy what you need to your hard disk, and provides details of any last-minute developments.

You can view the READ.ME file using the DOS TYPE command, as shown in the following example.

```
type d:\read.me | more
```

If your CD drive isn't the D: drive, replace `d:` in the example above with the appropriate letter. A prompt (`--MORE--`) appears at the bottom of the screen while there is more text for you to read. To scroll ahead, press any key when you're ready to continue.

CHAPTER

1

1

BASICS

These are wild times. PC horsepower has quietly increased to the point where effects you'd swear would take a high end graphics workstation to create can now be achieved by a person with a PC, a shareware ray tracer and a dream. The trick is translating that dream into code the ray tracer can handle.

```
DO WHILE INKEY$ = ""
```

and *INKEY$* becomes something other than a zero length string ("").

Polyray Version

The Polyray code for the TUMBLE animation is essentially the same as
TUMBLE.BAS. In fact it's somewhat simpler, since Polyray has a box primitive and simple vector notation for rotation. Box primitives allow you to call
up a box by specifying its opposite corners, instead of having to build six
sides with lines. Vector notation makes multidimensional operations as simple to use as addition and subtraction, relieving you of the chore of dealing
with each dimension (*x*, *y*, and *z* or *R*, *G*, and *B*) separately. A sample image
for the following Polyray data file is shown in Figure 1-2.

```
// A Tumbling Cube with Spheres

start_frame 0
end_frame 71
total_frames 72

outfile "TUMB"

define ang frame* 5

include "PLY\COLORS.INC"

viewpoint {
   from <0,0,-7>
   at <0,0,0>
   up <0,1,0>
   angle 40
   resolution 320,200
   aspect 1.433
   }

background SkyBlue

light white, <-5,5,-10>
light white, < 5,5,-10>

define pi 3.1415927
define rad pi / 180

define xrotate 2 * ang
define yrotate ang
define zrotate 90 * SIN(ang * rad)

define v1 < 1,  1,  1>
define v2 < 1,  1, -1>
define v3 < 1, -1,  1>
define v4 < 1, -1, -1>
```

```
define v5 <-1,  1,  1>
define v6 <-1,  1, -1>
define v7 <-1, -1,  1>
define v8 <-1, -1, -1>

object {
    object { box <-1,-1,-1>, <1,1,1> matte_white }
  + object { sphere v1, 0.4 shiny_red }
  + object { sphere v2, 0.4 shiny_orange }
  + object { sphere v3, 0.4 shiny_yellow }
  + object { sphere v4, 0.4 shiny_green }
  + object { sphere v5, 0.4 shiny_blue }
  + object { sphere v6, 0.4 shiny_cyan }
  + object { sphere v7, 0.4 shiny_magenta }
  + object { sphere v8, 0.4 shiny_coral }
  rotate <xrotate,yrotate,zrotate>
}
```

We use 72 frames that multiplied by 5° give 360° of motion during the animation and will return us to our starting point. The eight vertices of a unit cube are defined to specify where the spheres giving us depth cues should be placed, although for the ray traced version it's no longer needed because the cube is solid. A collective object is generated, composed of our box primitive and our spheres, and we rotate the lot with the rotate command.

Comments

QuickBasic simulation code usually translates painlessly to Polyray. Variables like

```
zrotate = 90 * SIN(angle * rad)
```

become

```
define zrotate 90 * SIN(ang * rad)
```

Figure 1-2 A tumbling cube done with Polyray

13

Note that *angle* is a reserved variable in Polyray, so we must replace it with *ang*. Polyray syntax is sometimes shorter than QuickBasic. The lengthy code for rotation in QuickBasic:

```
x0 = cubefixed(a).x
y0 = cubefixed(a).y
z0 = cubefixed(a).z

x1 = x0
y1 = y0 * COS(xrotate * rad) - z0 * SIN(xrotate * rad)
z1 = y0 * SIN(xrotate * rad) + z0 * COS(xrotate * rad)

x2 = z1 * SIN(yrotate * rad) + x1 * COS(yrotate * rad)
y2 = y1
z2 = z1 * COS(yrotate * rad) - x1 * SIN(yrotate * rad)

x3 = x2 * COS(zrotate * rad) - y2 * SIN(zrotate * rad)
y3 = x2 * SIN(zrotate * rad) + y2 * COS(zrotate * rad)
z3 = z2

cube(a).x = x3
cube(a).y = y3
cube(a).z = z3
```

condenses down to the single line in Polyray:

```
rotate <xrotate,yrotate,zrotate>
```

Vector operations like this are incredibly convenient inside Polyray. We'll use them frequently throughout the book.

1.2 How do I ...
Set a simple scene in motion?

You'll find the code for this in: PLY\CHAPTER1\COIN

Problem

Calculating the orientation and position of objects involved in multiple simultaneous motions could be a real nightmare. Something as simple as flipping a coin in the air requires linking a parabolic translation (the toss) to an independent rotation (the flip), and time sequencing the displacements could be a pain. Fortunately, Polyray has the ability to specify an object's motion, along with its shape and color, when it's defined. In fact, any time the object is called, additional motions can be assigned to it that simply add together to produce motions of arbitrary complexity.

This animation shows a metal coin being tossed in the air and it follows a parabolic path. As it flies, it flips about its own axis, revealing both sides. Around the outer perimeter of the coin are six small balls that circulate like the hands of a clock. This demonstrates how to generate motions that are nested three levels deep: (a) the coin flips, (b) the balls circulate, and (c) the whole thing follows a parabolic arc, as shown in Figure 1-3.

Technique

Animating objects requires changing their locations and orientations from frame to frame. While you *could* write separate scene description files for every single frame, Polyray's internal animation support makes it much simpler. Variables may be controlled by the frame counter, which is a variable called *frame* that increments by 1 every frame. A 30 frame animation is specified by including the following lines at the start of the animation:

```
start_frame 0
end_frame 29
total_frames 30
```

The *frame* variable will assume the values from 0 to 29. You may use this value directly or include it in a formula that in turn generates other values that can be used to control other objects for more complex motions.

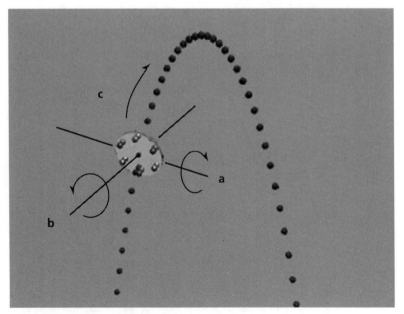

Figure 1-3 Coin flipping geometry

For example, a straight line linear motion of a sphere along the x axis would be:

```
object {
    sphere
    translate <frame, 0 0>
}
```

The *frame* variable increments once per frame, so this definition becomes

```
translate <1, 0 0>
translate <2, 0 0>
translate <3, 0 0>
...
```

and so on. To make this motion slower, you'd divide it by some number (e.g. *frame*/10). Then, the object would move 0.1 units each frame. To make our sphere oscillate back and forth along the x axis, you'd use *frame* in a sine function:

```
object {
    sphere
    translate <sin(frame/10), 0 0>
}
```

This would cause the position along the x axis to assume the values shown in Figure 1-4.

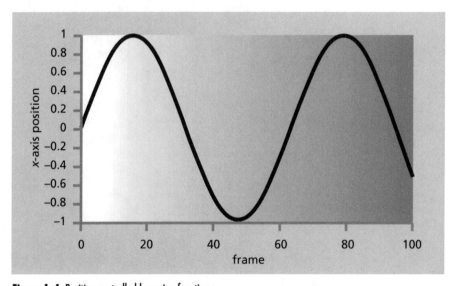

Figure 1-4 Position controlled by a sine function

Complex motions can be predefined in Polyray to keep the object definitions uncluttered:

```
define pi 3.14159
define rad pi/180

define staircase
        sin(5*frame*rad)/5 +
        sin(4*frame*rad)/4 +
        sin(3*frame*rad)/3 +
        sin(2*frame*rad)/2 +
        sin(1*frame*rad)/1

object {
   sphere
   translate <staircase, 0 0>
}
```

This would produce a wave form shown in Figure 1-5. If the axis running
from -2 to 2 in the figure defined the position of an object down a path, the
motion would resemble a typewriter carriage, (jerky forward motion, quick
return) for those of you old enough to remember typewriters.

Back to the animation at hand, we have three motions to define. Rotating
the balls on the face requires us to define them with the coin and set them in
motion prior to flipping the coin, otherwise they won't stick to the surface as
it moves. Flipping the coin will then be perpendicular to this rotation.
Tossing the coin in the air will be achieved using a parabolic arc, where the
effects of gravity slow the upward motion of the coin until it reaches a peak
then accelerates back down to earth, with a constant left to right translation
across the screen.

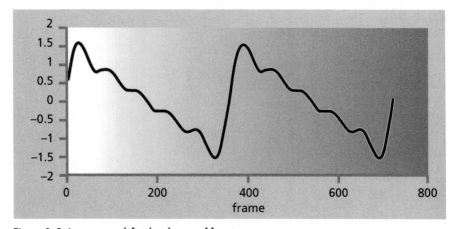

Figure 1-5 A ramp wave defined as the sum of five sine waves

Steps

To create the animation, we need to specify the following items:

- the number of frames

- the file names we want to use for the images (sequentially numbered)

- a viewpoint

- the camera's location

- what it's pointing at

- the resolution of the image

- a background color

- some lights

- `include` files containing colors and textures we plan to use

- any additional texture definitions not part of the `include` files

- the objects themselves

COIN.PI, the next listing, shows what these items look like before adding the objects.

```
// COIN.PI

start_frame 0
end_frame 29
total_frames 30
outfile "coin"

viewpoint {
   from <0,6,-16>
   at <0,0,0>
   up <0,1,0>
   angle 45
   resolution 320,200
   aspect 1.433
   }

background <0.439,0.576,0.859>      // a light bluish
light white, < 10,20, -10>         // a white light

include "\PLY\COLORS.INC"
```

```
define copper <0.72,0.45,0.20>

define reflective_copper
texture {
   surface {
      ambient copper, 0.2
      diffuse copper, 0.6
      specular copper, 0.8
      reflection copper, 0.9
      microfacet Phong 10
      }
   }
```

The Coin

The coin is constructed from three pieces: a short cylinder capped by two discs, centered on the origin (see Figure 1-6). Cylinders are defined by specifying the centers of both ends and a radius (in this case, the radius is 8 units). Cylinders are not capped, so we must define both faces of the coin as two discs.

Discs are created by specifying their centers, a *surface_normal* (a vector perpendicular to the plane of the disc), and a radius. The next listing collects these objects together into a single object by adding their component parts together.

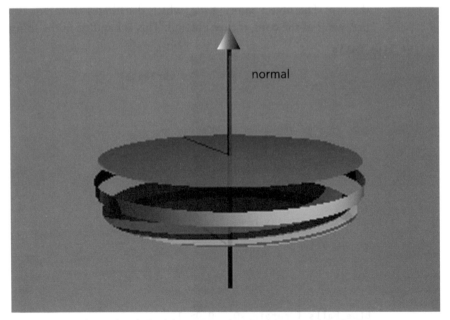

Figure 1-6 Two discs and a cylinder define our coin. Note the surface normals for the discs

rendering. Recall that *wire_frame* is specified in the POLYRAY.INI file or as a command line option. A balance must be reached between being close enough to see the balls rotate on the face of the coin and catching the arc motion as well. The coin will move linearly along the *x* axis and assume an upside down parabolic path along the *y* axis. This is handled as follows:

```
// figured out manually

define ymin   -63
define ymax    35
define xmin   -35
define xmax    35

define yrange ymax - ymin
define height -yrange * ((frame_normal) ^ 2) +ymax
define dist   frame_normal*xmax

object {
   flipping_coin { translate <dist,height,0> }
}
```

Now that the frame count doesn't directly impact the motion, render COIN.PI with *total_frames* of 75 and 150 and watch the action.

How It Works

To reiterate the motion-layering concept, if you place an object in motion in its initial definition, when it's called later on, that motion comes along. We define the coin as a *flipping_coin* and the balls as *many_balls* that are already in motion, and let Polyray deal with the low-level details. When we toss the coin, it's a spinning, flipping coin. The ability to nest motions in this manner makes producing complex multifaceted motions a breeze.

Variations

Now that we have a flipping coin defined, we can call it up many times and make lots of them. To avoid making them look like they're all on a rotisserie, start them off at different times and locations. For example, define a series of offsets (*off1, off2, ...*), include them in copies of the description for the height and position of the coin, and you'll end up making a lot of coins that are time-shifted from each other. Time shifting is accomplished by adding a little extra to the variables we use to control our object:

```
define off1   -0.1
define heig1 -yrange * ((frame_normal+off1) ^ 2) +ymax
define dist1 (frame_normal+off1)*xmax
```

```
define off2  0.1
define heig2 -yrange * ((frame_normal+off2) ^ 2) +ymax
define dist2 (frame_normal+off2)*xmax

define off3  0.3
define heig3 -yrange * ((frame_normal+off3) ^ 2) +ymax
define dist3 (frame_normal+off3)*xmax

define off4  0.5
define heig4 -yrange * ((frame_normal+off4) ^ 2) +ymax
define dist4 (frame_normal+off4)*xmax

define off4  0.7
define heig5 -yrange * ((frame_normal+off5) ^ 2) +ymax
define dist5 (frame_normal+off5)*xmax

object {flipping_coin { translate <dist1,heig1,0> }}
object {flipping_coin { translate <dist2,heig2,0> }}
object {flipping_coin { translate <dist3,heig3,0> }}
object {flipping_coin { translate <dist4,heig4,0> }}
object {flipping_coin { translate <dist5,heig5,0> }}
```

Try making one coin solid and fade the others (change their textures to more transparent ones) so that the coin leaves trails. This can also be accomplished by post processing with DTA. Move the balls in and out as the coin rotates. Change their size. Move the camera through the scene to produce depth cues. With appropriate collision detection, a particle systems animation could be written. We'll cover particle systems in Chapter 5, *Particle Systems*.

CHAPTER 2

continued from previous page

```
PRINT "frames = "; n; " final angle = "; a - speed / r4
PRINT USING "final location <###.#####, ###.#####, ###.#####>"; x, y, z
CLOSE #1

SUB rotate (d, e, f)

    x0 = d
    y0 = e
    z0 = f

    x1 = x0
    y1 = y0 * COS(xrotate * rad) - z0 * SIN(xrotate * rad)
    z1 = y0 * SIN(xrotate * rad) + z0 * COS(xrotate * rad)

    x2 = z1 * SIN(yrotate * rad) + x1 * COS(yrotate * rad)
    y2 = y1
    z2 = z1 * COS(yrotate * rad) - x1 * SIN(yrotate * rad)

    x3 = x2 * COS(zrotate * rad) - y2 * SIN(zrotate * rad)
    y3 = x2 * SIN(zrotate * rad) + y2 * COS(zrotate * rad)
    z3 = z2

    d = x3
    e = y3
    f = z3

END SUB
```

Step 3

To use the include file this program generates, add the following lines to the Polyray listing in the next section:

```
light white*0.5, <20,35,40>
include "path.inc"
```

Then add the two fixed vantage points—one for the whole path, the other for focusing on the valley—with the following viewpoint code.

```
// set up the camera
viewpoint {
   from <20,30,40>  // to see the whole path
   at <0,5,0>
//   from <1,15,1>  // to see the valley focal point
//   at <0,5,0>
   up <0,1,0>
   angle 35
   resolution 320,240
   aspect 1.33
   }
```

Polyray Data File

The Polyray translation follows pretty much the same style as the QuickBasic simulation code shown here in SWOOP.PI.

```
// SWOOP.PI

// Tangent Pattern Flyover

start_frame 0
end_frame 231
total_frames 232

outfile swoop

define pi 3.1415927
define rad pi/180

define r1 12
define r2 8
define r3 r1 - r2
define r4 r3/2
define speed 20

define align <0,125,0>

define focus <-0.3,0.75,-0.3>
define origin <0,0,0>

if (frame==start_frame) {
   static define a 0
   static define was_at rotate(<-0.2587,0,0.21577>,-align)
   static define fromvect focus
}

// stage 1

if (a < 360) {
   define norm a / 360
   define r (1 - norm) * r2 + norm * r1
   define x1 r * COS(a * rad) - r2
   define z1 r * SIN(a * rad)
   static define a a + speed / r
}

// stage 2
if (a>359 && a< 540) {
   define x1 r3 * COS(a * rad)
   define z1 r3 * SIN(a * rad)
   static define a a + speed / r3
}

// stage 3
```

continued on next page

continued from previous page

```
if (a >539 && a <720) {
    define x1   r4 * COS(a * rad) - r4
    define z1   r4 * SIN(a * rad)
    static define a a + speed / r4
}

define center1 240
define width1 80
define height1 15

define center2 0
define width2 100
define height2 2

define  y1 height1 * (1 / (EXP(((a - center1) / width1) ^ 2)))
define cam height2 * (1 / (EXP(((a - center2) / width2) ^ 2)))

static define fromvect <x1,y1,z1>
define atvect (cam * ((fromvect-was_at) + fromvect) + (1 - cam) * origin)
static define was_at fromvect

// Set up the camera
viewpoint {
    from rotate(fromvect,align)+focus
    at rotate(atvect,align)+focus
    up <0,1,0>
    angle 35
    resolution 320,240
    aspect 1.33
}

// Get various surface finishes
include "\ply\colors.inc"

define mountain_colors
texture {
    noise surface {
        ambient 0.25
        diffuse 0.8
        specular 0.2
        position_fn 1
        color_map(
            [-1.28,-0.66, MidnightBlue, Navy]
            [-0.66,-0.30, Navy, Blue]
            [-0.30, 0.00, Blue, MediumBlue]
            [ 0.00, 0.20, ForestGreen, SpringGreen]
            [ 0.20, 0.40, SpringGreen, Gold]
            [ 0.40, 0.80, Gold, GoldenRod]
            [ 0.80, 1.28, GoldenRod, Gray])
        }
    rotate <0, 0, 90>
    }
```

```
// Set up background color & lights
background MidnightBlue
spot_light <1.0,1.0,1.0>, <-20,10,-20>, <0,0,0>, 3, 25, 45
spot_light <1.0,1.0,1.0>, <20,10,-20>, <0,0,0>, 3, 25, 45

define ra (x^2+z^2)^0.5
define HFn (sin(pi * tan(x) + pi * tan(z))) / ra

define detail 200

// Define a patterned surface

   object {
      smooth_height_fn detail, detail, -15, 15, -15, 15, HFn
      mountain_colors
   }

// The following code was used to view the path
// remove the comment slashes (//) to use it
// Set up the camera

//viewpoint {
//   from <20,30,-40>  // to see the whole path
//   at <0,5,0>
////   from <1,15,1>  // to see the valley focal point
////   at <0,5,0>
//   up <0,1,0>
//   angle 35
//   resolution 640,480
//   aspect 1.33
//   }

//include "path.inc"
//light white, <20,35,40>
```

How It Works

The frame count goes from 0 to 231, but the motivating variable is actually *a,* the angle count, which goes from 0 to 720. Polyray uses the key word *static* to define variables whose values stick around from frame to frame, allowing us to build upon their previous values to create subsequent ones.

There are three stages in the Polyray file, as in the QuickBasic code, that generate the spiraling path of various radii under control of the angle counter *a.* The two Gaussian functions specify *y1,* the height of the path above the surface as a function of the angle, and *cam,* the proportioning of where the camera is pointing, between a fixed viewpoint and one that is moving down the path. The fixed viewpoint is the origin; the one moving down the path is given by:

```
((fromvect-was_at) + fromvect)
```

which adds the current path direction to the current camera location to generate a view that follows the path. These two are proportionally added depending on the *cam* value to generate the *atvect*.

```
define atvect (cam * ((fromvect-was_at) + fromvect) + (1 - cam) * origin)
```

These variables *fromvect* and *atvect* specify the camera position and what the camera looks at. Next, the path must be rotated to align it with the surface features, which is done "on the fly" inside the viewpoint code. After the rotation, the entire path is offset by the vector *focus* to move it into the center of the valley on the surface.

After calculating *fromvect* and *atvect, was_at* is set to *fromvect* to be used in the next frame to generate the current camera path. This brings up one issue. How is the first frame variable *was_at* determined? It's done manually in the simulation code.

```
if (frame==start_frame) {
    static define a 0
    static define was_at rotate(<-0.2587,0,0.21577>,-align)
    static define fromvect focus
}
```

We run the entire simulation, and print out the coordinates of the camera in the last frame. The major difference between the QuickBasic code and the Polyray code is that QuickBasic rotates the path on the fly, while the Polyray code rotates the path at the end, in the viewpoint block. The last PRINT statement in the simulation code gives the rotated value for the last position of the camera. Since the animation loops, this is the *was_at* value for the first frame, but before Polyray can use it, we must de-rotate it by the angle *-align*.

Mountain_colors is a texture map using a linear gradient ranging from -1.28 to 1.28, which varies from blue to green to tan to white. Color maps default to running left to right in the *x-z* plane. This map needs to be tipped on its side using a 90° rotation to make it run up and down, which allows us to highlight variations in surface height with different colors.

The smooth heightfield has a variable *detail* that allows us to specify how detailed we want the heightfield to be. More detail takes more memory, more time, and can dramatically change the look of a surface as compared to a less detailed surface, since the heightfield function is not antialiased. The heightfield function does not use the average value for the controlling function over an area, but rather the value at a specific point on the surface. If the function defining the surface has elements whose dimensions are smaller than the sampling grid defined by detail, spurious details may appear. The height and exact position of the foothills and the mountain change depending on the level of detail that is used.

Comments

For all the effort we went through to smooth the focal point transition during the flythrough, we really only moved it away from the center of the valley. There's still a pretty substantial lurch as the camera swings around to point back at the mountain. A shock absorber approach, one that would limit the rate of change in the angular rotation of the camera to some maximum value, would probably do a better job. It requires keeping track of the angular change, an error term between where the code wants the camera to point and where it's actually pointing, and an if-else construction to select between the two. This animation is already complicated enough, however, so we'll leave it as it is for now. Don't let this stop you from trying it.

2.2 How do I...
Show a spaceship being launched down a flight tube?

You'll find the code for this in: PLY\CHAPTER2\ROCKET

Problem

Animations involving long linear camera motions are expensive from a modeling standpoint, since all the work required to generate something interesting in front of the camera is lost as soon as the camera passes by the objects. We may only get to see the entire model at the beginning of the animation. For repetitive structures like hallways or tunnels, we can move parts of the model back up in front of the camera after we pass them. This makes long structures appear to go on forever. It's known as *treadmilling.*

Technique

We'll create a simulation of the animation without treadmilling in order to examine timing and frame count, do a Polyray animation from this information, and then add treadmilling and chaser lights. The basic concept of this animation is to watch a rocket pass closely by the camera and fly out the end of a launch tube.

Steps

We build a tunnel from the intersection of crossed cylinders, and trolley the camera from one end of the tunnel to the other. Halfway through the animation, a rocket ship launched from some distance behind the camera at

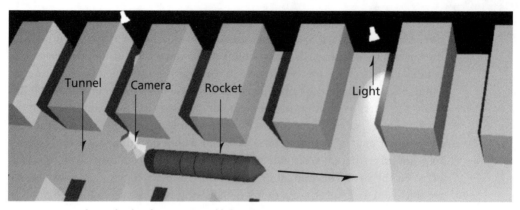

Figure 2-8 Launch tunnel with rocket, camera, and light source

twice its speed overtakes it and we watch as the rocket majestically passes and flies out the end of the tunnel (Figure 2-8).

We can simulate this motion with the following QuickBasic code. It shows an outside view of the action to give us a feel for the timing and choreography.

```
' ROCKET1.BAS
' Polyray Rocket Launch Animation Simulation

SCREEN 12
WINDOW (-32, -24)-(32, 24)

'the tunnel - alternating tall and square boxes
FOR x = -15 TO 16
   IF x MOD 2 = 0 THEN
      LINE (x - .5, -2)-(x + .5, 2), 15, B
   ELSE
      LINE (x - .5, -.5)-(x + .5, .5), 15, B
   END IF
NEXT x

'  some constants - they stay fixed but follow the
'  syntax of the changing variables

cameray = .2    ' camera y-offset
lookaty = 0     ' look at y-offset
rockety = 0     ' rocket y-offset

ocy = cameray   ' old camera y-offset
oly = lookaty   ' old look at y-offest
ory = rockety   ' old rocket y-offset

totalframes = 200

FOR frame = 0 TO totalframes
   norm = frame / totalframes     ' frame normal - 0 to 1
```

```
   cameraz = -15 + 30 * norm    ' camera goes from -15 to 15
   lookatz = -10 + 30 * norm    ' look at leads the camera by 5
   rocketz = -30 + 60 * norm    ' rocket goes from -30 to 30

   'undraw
   FOR section = -4 TO 4
      LINE (orz - .4 + section, ory - .05)-
      (orz + .4 + section, ory + .05), 0, BF
   NEXT section

   CIRCLE (ocz, ocy), .2, 0
   CIRCLE (olz, oly), .2, 0


   'draw
   FOR section = -4 TO 4
      LINE (rocketz - .4 + section, rockety - .05)-
      (rocketz + .4 + section, rockety + .05), 4, BF
   NEXT section

   CIRCLE (cameraz, cameray), .2, 4
   CIRCLE (lookatz, lookaty), .2, 2

   'save
   orz = rocketz
   ocz = cameraz
   olz = lookatz

   ' a pause loop to slow it down for viewing
   FOR w = 1 TO 10000: NEXT w
NEXT frame
```

The Polyray code gives us the view from the camera's perspective. The launch tunnel is comprised of 33 short cylinders staggered at right angles to the flight path. A central cylinder is drilled through all of their centers to define the flight tube (Figure 2-9).

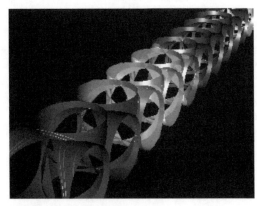

Figure 2-9 Our rocket launch tunnel

ROCK1.PI, the next listing, builds the rocket out of nine cylinders. Small spaces defined by the variable *slot* separate the cylinders. The rocket passes over a light in the center of the tunnel, and the light that leaks out through the slots shows up as stripes on the walls of the launch tube.

```
// ROCK1.PI
start_frame 0
end_frame 150
total_frames 90   //  don't worry about this.

outfile rock
include "\PLY\COLORS.INC"

define norm frame/total_frames
define rocketz -40 + frame/3

viewpoint {
   from  <0.20, 0.20,-14+14*norm>
   up    <0, 1, 0>
   at    <0,0.0,-10+14*norm>
   angle 25
   resolution 160,120
   aspect 1.33
   }


// the red rocket

define slot 0.47
define section
   object {
      cylinder <0,0,-0.5+slot>,<0,0, 0.5-slot>,0.2
      }

define t1 <0,0,-4+rocketz>
define t2 <0,0,-3+rocketz>
define t3 <0,0,-2+rocketz>
define t4 <0,0,-1+rocketz>
define t5 <0,0, 0+rocketz>
define t6 <0,0, 1+rocketz>
define t7 <0,0, 2+rocketz>
define t8 <0,0, 3+rocketz>
define t9 <0,0, 4+rocketz>

define rocket
object {
      object { section translate t1 }
    + object { section translate t2 }
    + object { section translate t3 }
    + object { section translate t4 }
    + object { section translate t5 }
    + object { section translate t6 }
    + object { section translate t7 }
```

```
   + object { section translate t8 }
   + object { section translate t9 }
   + object { cone <0, 0, 0>, 0.2, <0, 0, 1>, 0 translate t9+<0,0,0.5>}
  shiny_red
  }


light <0,0,0>
light <-5, 0, 10>
light < 5, 0, 10>


background midnightblue

define launch_tube
   object {
// the side chambers
      object { cylinder <-2, 0,-16>, < 2, 0,-16>, 1 }
    + object { cylinder < 0,-2,-15>, < 0, 2,-15>, 1 }
    + object { cylinder <-2, 0,-14>, < 2, 0,-14>, 1 }
    + object { cylinder < 0,-2,-13>, < 0, 2,-13>, 1 }
    + object { cylinder <-2, 0,-12>, < 2, 0,-12>, 1 }
    + object { cylinder < 0,-2,-11>, < 0, 2,-11>, 1 }
    + object { cylinder <-2, 0,-10>, < 2, 0,-10>, 1 }
    + object { cylinder < 0,-2, -9>, < 0, 2, -9>, 1 }
    + object { cylinder <-2, 0, -8>, < 2, 0, -8>, 1 }
    + object { cylinder < 0,-2, -7>, < 0, 2, -7>, 1 }
    + object { cylinder <-2, 0, -6>, < 2, 0, -6>, 1 }
    + object { cylinder < 0,-2, -5>, < 0, 2, -5>, 1 }
    + object { cylinder <-2, 0, -4>, < 2, 0, -4>, 1 }
    + object { cylinder < 0,-2, -3>, < 0, 2, -3>, 1 }
    + object { cylinder <-2, 0, -2>, < 2, 0, -2>, 1 }
    + object { cylinder < 0,-2,  1>, < 0, 2,  1>, 1 }
    + object { cylinder <-2, 0,  0>, < 2, 0,  0>, 1 }
    + object { cylinder < 0,-2,  1>, < 0, 2,  1>, 1 }
    + object { cylinder <-2, 0,  2>, < 2, 0,  2>, 1 }
    + object { cylinder < 0,-2,  3>, < 0, 2,  3>, 1 }
    + object { cylinder <-2, 0,  4>, < 2, 0,  4>, 1 }
    + object { cylinder < 0,-2,  5>, < 0, 2,  5>, 1 }
    + object { cylinder <-2, 0,  6>, < 2, 0,  6>, 1 }
    + object { cylinder < 0,-2,  7>, < 0, 2,  7>, 1 }
    + object { cylinder <-2, 0,  8>, < 2, 0,  8>, 1 }
    + object { cylinder < 0,-2,  9>, < 0, 2,  9>, 1 }
    + object { cylinder <-2, 0, 10>, < 2, 0, 10>, 1 }
    + object { cylinder < 0,-2, 11>, < 0, 2, 11>, 1 }
    + object { cylinder <-2, 0, 12>, < 2, 0, 12>, 1 }
    + object { cylinder < 0,-2, 13>, < 0, 2, 13>, 1 }
    + object { cylinder <-2, 0, 14>, < 2, 0, 14>, 1 }
    + object { cylinder < 0,-2, 15>, < 0, 2, 15>, 1 }
    + object { cylinder <-2, 0, 16>, < 2, 0, 16>, 1 }

    & ~object {cylinder < 0, 0,-18>, < 0, 0, 18>, 1}
    texture {surface {color coral ambient 0.3 diffuse 0.8}}
  }

launch_tube
```

Treadmilling the Model

In order to treadmill the cylindrical sections of the launch tube, we define a variable called *nudge* that shifts the entire tunnel towards the camera a little bit each frame. It uses modulo math, that is, the remainder of one number divided by another number. Since the other number is 20, it repeats every 20 frames. With the repeating units of the tunnel being two units apart, and the fact that we're dividing the modulo term by 10, the tunnel also lines up with its original orientation every 20 frames. Here's how:

```
define nudge 2 - fmod(frame,20) / 10
define launch_tube
   object {
// The side chambers
      object { cylinder <-1.2, 0,-18+nudge>, < 1.2, 0,-18+nudge>, 1 }
    + object { cylinder < 0,-1.2,-17+nudge>, < 0, 1.2,-17+nudge>, 1 }
    + object { cylinder <-1.2, 0,-16+nudge>, < 1.2, 0,-16+nudge>, 1 }
    ...
```

This dramatically changes the way we generate the apparent motion. Before, we moved the camera down the tunnel. Now we'll hold the camera steady, move the tunnel towards us and the rocket away from us, but from the camera's perspective, it looks exactly the same as the previous animation. The main difference is that the tunnel appears to go on forever, while the model is in fact of finite length, with a (better still) finite rendering time.

Chaser Lights

Although the light leaking through the slots in the rocket in the previous animation was a nice effect, it would fail to seriously stun anyone. The desired effect was much more dramatic: moving lights tugging our rocket forward like the powerful magnetic forces in a linear accelerator.

Let's use chasers. These are a series of moving lights that travel down the length of the tube, as shown by lines in Figure 2-10. The lines actually represent four spotlights surrounding the launch tube, shining through the holes at an angle.

ROCKETZ.BAS, shown in the following code, shows the chaser lights as they relate to the launch tube. Remember, the tube's being pulled one way, the rocket's moving out the other way, and the camera's staying put. The ends of this simulation are a bit rough, but it gives you a pretty good idea of the motion. Use modulo math again to get a linear displacement that repeats, in this case every 16 frames.

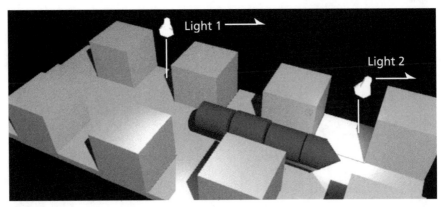

Figure 2-10 Vertical lines show the positions of chaser lights. They move left to right during the animation

```
' ROCKETZ.BAS
SCREEN 12
WINDOW (-32, -24)-(32, 24)

' a tunnel conveyor belt
FOR frame = 0 TO 200
   nudge = 2 - (frame MOD 20) / 10
   LOCATE 10, 38: PRINT USING "### "; frame
' pause code-use as needed
   FOR w = 1 TO 10000: NEXT w

   'the tunnel
   FOR px = -15 TO 16
   'undraw
      ox = px + nudge + .1
      IF px MOD 2 = 0 THEN
         LINE (ox - .5, -2)-(ox + .5, 2), 0, B
      ELSE
         LINE (ox - .5, -.5)-(ox + .5, .5), 0, B
      END IF

   'draw
      x = px + nudge
      IF px MOD 2 = 0 THEN
         LINE (x - .5, -2)-(x + .5, 2), 15, B
      ELSE
         LINE (x - .5, -.5)-(x + .5, .5), 15, B
      END IF
   NEXT px

   'the ship
   rocketx = -40 + frame / 3

   'undraw
```

continued on next page

53

continued from previous page

```
   FOR section = -4 TO 4
     LINE (orx - .4 + section, ory - .05)-
     (orx + .4 + section, ory + .05), 0, BF
   NEXT section

   'draw
   FOR section = -4 TO 4
     LINE (rocketx - .4 + section, rockety - .05)-
     (rocketx + .4 + section, rockety + .05), 4, BF
   NEXT section

   'save
   orx = rocketx
   ory = rockety

   'AAAAAAAAAAAAAAAAAAAAAAAAAAAAAAAAAAAAAAAAAAAAAAAAAAAAA
   'traveling "chaser" lights using modulo math again
   'VVVVVVVVVVVVVVVVVVVVVVVVVVVVVVVVVVVVVVVVVVVVVVVVVVVVVV

   trl1 = -16 + frame MOD 16
   trl2 = 0 + frame MOD 16

   LINE (trl1, -5)-(trl1, 5), count
   LINE (trl2, -5)-(trl2, 5), count

   IF trl2 = 0 THEN count = count + 1

NEXT frame
```

Polyray Data File

The final animation sequence (ROCKET.PI) can either hold the camera steady inside the tube, or shift from the outside to the inside of the launch tube just to show off how good the tunnel looks from the outside. This second animation doesn't loop smoothly, so that code (the lines following the comment "shifting point of view") has been commented out, but you may wish to try it out. It's an exponential shift between two viewpoints $v0$ and $v1$.

```
// ROCKET.PI - Rocket Launching Animation

start_frame 0
end_frame 160
total_frames 160

outfile rock
include "..\colors.inc"

// shifting point of view - next 4 lines
```

```
// define v0 <10,10,-30>
// define v1 <0.45,0.35,-16>
// define shift 1/exp(frame/16)
// define v2 shift*v0+(1-shift)*v1

// steady point of view
   define v2 <0.45,0.35,-16>

viewpoint {
   from v2
   at <0,0,-12>
   up <0, 1, 0>
   angle 25
   resolution 320,200
   aspect 1.33
   }


// The ROCKET Definition Code

define slot 0.02
define section
   object {
       cylinder <0,0,-0.5+slot>,<0,0, 0.5-slot>,0.2
       }

define rocketz -40 + frame / 3

define t1 <0,0,-4+rocketz>
define t2 <0,0,-3+rocketz>
define t3 <0,0,-2+rocketz>
define t4 <0,0,-1+rocketz>
define t5 <0,0, 0+rocketz>
define t6 <0,0, 1+rocketz>
define t7 <0,0, 2+rocketz>
define t8 <0,0, 3+rocketz>
define t9 <0,0, 4+rocketz>

define rocket
object {
     object { section translate t1 }
   + object { section translate t2 }
   + object { section translate t3 }
   + object { section translate t4 }
   + object { section translate t5 }
   + object { section translate t6 }
   + object { section translate t7 }
   + object { section translate t8 }
   + object { section translate t9 }
   + object { cone <0, 0, 0>, 0.2, <0, 0, 1>, 0 translate t9+<0,0,0.5>}
  shiny_red
  }

  rocket
```

continued on next page

continued from previous page

```
// engine inside rocket

light <1,1,2>,t1
object {
   sphere t1,0.2
   shading_flags 32+8+4+2+1
}

//light t2
//light t3
//light t4
light t5
//light t6
//light t7
//light t8
light t9


background midnightblue

define nudge 2 - fmod(frame,20) / 10
define launch_tube
   object {
// The side chambers
       object { cylinder <-1.2, 0,-18+nudge>, < 1.2, 0,-18+nudge>, 1 }
     + object { cylinder < 0,-1.2,-17+nudge>, < 0, 1.2,-17+nudge>, 1 }
     + object { cylinder <-1.2, 0,-16+nudge>, < 1.2, 0,-16+nudge>, 1 }
     + object { cylinder < 0,-1.2,-15+nudge>, < 0, 1.2,-15+nudge>, 1 }
     + object { cylinder <-1.2, 0,-14+nudge>, < 1.2, 0,-14+nudge>, 1 }
     + object { cylinder < 0,-1.2,-13+nudge>, < 0, 1.2,-13+nudge>, 1 }
     + object { cylinder <-1.2, 0,-12+nudge>, < 1.2, 0,-12+nudge>, 1 }
     + object { cylinder < 0,-1.2,-11+nudge>, < 0, 1.2,-11+nudge>, 1 }
     + object { cylinder <-1.2, 0,-10+nudge>, < 1.2, 0,-10+nudge>, 1 }
     + object { cylinder < 0,-1.2, -9+nudge>, < 0, 1.2, -9+nudge>, 1 }
     + object { cylinder <-1.2, 0, -8+nudge>, < 1.2, 0, -8+nudge>, 1 }
     + object { cylinder < 0,-1.2, -7+nudge>, < 0, 1.2, -7+nudge>, 1 }
     + object { cylinder <-1.2, 0, -6+nudge>, < 1.2, 0, -6+nudge>, 1 }
     + object { cylinder < 0,-1.2, -5+nudge>, < 0, 1.2, -5+nudge>, 1 }
     + object { cylinder <-1.2, 0, -4+nudge>, < 1.2, 0, -4+nudge>, 1 }
     + object { cylinder < 0,-1.2, -3+nudge>, < 0, 1.2, -3+nudge>, 1 }
     + object { cylinder <-1.2, 0, -2+nudge>, < 1.2, 0, -2+nudge>, 1 }
     + object { cylinder < 0,-1.2,  1+nudge>, < 0, 1.2,  1+nudge>, 1 }
     + object { cylinder <-1.2, 0,  0+nudge>, < 1.2, 0,  0+nudge>, 1 }
     + object { cylinder < 0,-1.2,  1+nudge>, < 0, 1.2,  1+nudge>, 1 }
     + object { cylinder <-1.2, 0,  2+nudge>, < 1.2, 0,  2+nudge>, 1 }
     + object { cylinder < 0,-1.2,  3+nudge>, < 0, 1.2,  3+nudge>, 1 }
     + object { cylinder <-1.2, 0,  4+nudge>, < 1.2, 0,  4+nudge>, 1 }
     + object { cylinder < 0,-1.2,  5+nudge>, < 0, 1.2,  5+nudge>, 1 }
     + object { cylinder <-1.2, 0,  6+nudge>, < 1.2, 0,  6+nudge>, 1 }
     + object { cylinder < 0,-1.2,  7+nudge>, < 0, 1.2,  7+nudge>, 1 }
     + object { cylinder <-1.2, 0,  8+nudge>, < 1.2, 0,  8+nudge>, 1 }
     + object { cylinder < 0,-1.2,  9+nudge>, < 0, 1.2,  9+nudge>, 1 }
     + object { cylinder <-1.2, 0, 10+nudge>, < 1.2, 0, 10+nudge>, 1 }
     + object { cylinder < 0,-1.2, 11+nudge>, < 0, 1.2, 11+nudge>, 1 }
```

```
  + object { cylinder <-1.2, 0, 12+nudge>, < 1.2, 0, 12+nudge>, 1 }
  + object { cylinder < 0,-1.2, 13+nudge>, < 0, 1.2, 13+nudge>, 1 }
  + object { cylinder <-1.2, 0, 14+nudge>, < 1.2, 0, 14+nudge>, 1 }
  + object { cylinder < 0,-1.2, 15+nudge>, < 0, 1.2, 15+nudge>, 1 }
  + object { cylinder <-1.2, 0, 16+nudge>, < 1.2, 0, 16+nudge>, 1 }

  & ~object {cylinder < 0, 0,-20>, < 0, 0, 20>, 1}
  texture {surface {color coral ambient 0.3 diffuse 0.8}}
}

launch_tube

// chaser lights

define trl1 -20 + fmod(frame,16)+nudge
define trl2  -4 + fmod(frame,16)+nudge

define pi 3.14159

spot_light white,<10,0,trl1-5>,<0,0,trl1>,3,5,18
spot_light white,<0,10,trl1-5>,<0,0,trl1>,3,5,18
spot_light white,<-10,0,trl1-5>,<0,0,trl1>,3,5,18
spot_light white,<0,-10,trl1-5>,<0,0,trl1>,3,5,18

spot_light white,<10,0,trl2-5>,<0,0,trl2>,3,5,18
spot_light white,<0,10,trl2-5>,<0,0,trl2>,3,5,18
spot_light white,<-10,0,trl2-5>,<0,0,trl2>,3,5,18
spot_light white,<0,-10,trl2-5>,<0,0,trl2>,3,5,18
```

How It Works

The fun begins with the structured definition of the rocket. It is constructed in stages from cylinders one unit long (minus the slot) centered on the origin, 0.2 units in diameter, that we call *section*. The variable *rocketz* establishes the forward motion of the rocket along the z axis under the control of the frame counter. We define nine points based on *rocketz* strung out in a line, *t1 – t9*, which specify the offsets for each section of the rocket. We make nine copies of the original *section* plus a nose cone, paint it red and call it *rocket* (Figure 2-11). The engine is a bluish light inside a sphere traveling along inside the

Figure 2-11 Our rocket

continued from previous page

```
    if (phz > 0 && 5 > (5 - moving)) {
        define x5 8 * cos(ang * rad) + 5 * 2 - 6
        define y5 8 * sin(ang * rad) + 8
    }
    else {
        define x5 5 * 2 - 6
        define y5 0
    }

    if (phz < 0 && 5 < (moving + 1)) {
        define x5 8 * cos(ang * rad) + 5 * 2 - 6
        define y5 8 * sin(ang * rad) + 8
    }

    define z 0

    object { sphere <x1,y1,z>,1 shiny_blue }
    object { sphere <x2,y2,z>,1 shiny_blue }
    object { sphere <x3,y3,z>,1 shiny_blue }
    object { sphere <x4,y4,z>,1 shiny_blue }
    object { sphere <x5,y5,z>,1 shiny_blue }

    object { cylinder <x1,y1+1,z>,<1*2-6,8,0>,0.25 shiny_coral }
    object { cylinder <x2,y2+1,z>,<2*2-6,8,0>,0.25 shiny_coral }
    object { cylinder <x3,y3+1,z>,<3*2-6,8,0>,0.25 shiny_coral }
    object { cylinder <x4,y4+1,z>,<4*2-6,8,0>,0.25 shiny_coral }
    object { cylinder <x5,y5+1,z>,<5*2-6,8,0>,0.25 shiny_coral }

    static define t t+10
    if (fmod(t,360)==0) static define moving moving+1
```

How It Works

Each ball is controlled by its own *if-else* block. We "unrolled" the loop in the QuickBasic code and hard-coded the decision values one at a time. For example, the code controlling ball 5 is:

```
if (phz > 0 && 5 > (5 - moving))
```

The variable *t* adds another swinging ball every 36 frames. For a 180 frame animation, we start with one ball swinging, and end up with five balls swinging. Since the balls will all be at rest at the beginning and end of the animation, it loops nicely, although the number of balls swinging goes 1-2-3-4-5-1-2-3-4-5... The jump between five and one balls moving is disconcerting. It would feel better if the number of balls moving changed by only one each cycle. Using the @list feature in DTA, we can force the animation to loop 1-2-3-4-5-4-3-2-1-2-3-4-5... by creating a list file that uses frames 0-179, then 108-143, 72-107, and 36-71. Otherwise, the code is identical to the QuickBasic version. Single cylinders are used as our string to attach the balls to an invisible frame.

Improving the Model

We've got the basic motion. Now we need to build a better frame to hold the balls. The rods extending up out of the balls are too thick, they need to be more like threads, and there needs to be two of them attached to parallel supports above the balls to keep them centered. We'll end up with your basic V shape.

Flapping Wings

For grins, let's make the support frame V flap its wings like a bird. A flap can be created as an asymmetrical wave form, with a slow smooth upward motion followed by a rapid downward motion, as illustrated in the wave form in Figure 2-14.

This is generated by periodically adding a hump (a Gaussian function) to a sine wave. The height of the balls attached to the wings should follow this periodic motion, but in the opposite direction. When the wings are moving down and spreading apart, the balls should be moving up. The following program (FLAP.BAS) draws the wave form at the bottom of Figure 2-14, pauses, then flaps the frame at the top of the figure.

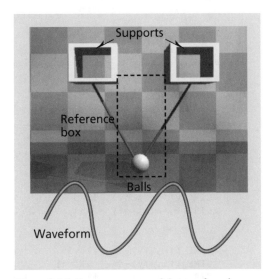

Figure 2-14 Flapping supports and the wave form they follow. The box was added as a spatial reference

```
' FLAP.BAS
SCREEN 12
WINDOW (-16, -12)-(16, 12)

pi = 3.14159
rad = pi / 180
frame = -16

'show the waveform

FOR angle = -360 TO 360 STEP 1
        x = angle / 30
        w = 10 * COS(angle * rad)
        z = EXP(1.6 * (1 + COS((angle - 80) * rad)))
        y = w + z
        IF angle = -360 THEN PSET (x, y / 5) ELSE LINE -(x, y / 5)
NEXT angle

DO WHILE INKEY$ = "": LOOP
CLS

' a reference box
LINE (-4, 0)-(4, 8), , B

DO WHILE INKEY$ = ""        ' go until a key is pressed
  t = t + 10                ' time step size

' ==================The Assymetric Waveform===================
        w = 10 * COS(t * rad)                   ' periodic motion
        z = EXP(1.6 * (1 + COS((t - 80) * rad))) ' periodic hump

        phz = w + z                             ' add 'em together
        ang = 45 + phz                          ' shift the phase
' ============================================================
        x = 8 * COS(ang * rad)
        y = 8 * SIN(ang * rad) + 2
        fx = 0
        fy = -4 * SIN(ang * rad) + 4

    ' undraw
        LINE (ofx, ofy)-(ox, oy), 0
        LINE (ofx, ofy)-(-ox, oy), 0
        CIRCLE (ox, oy), 1, 0
        CIRCLE (-ox, oy), 1, 0
        CIRCLE (ofx, ofy - .5), .5, 0

    ' draw
        LINE (fx, fy)-(x, y), 15        ' draw the current screen
        LINE (fx, fy)-(-x, y), 15       ' draw the current screen
        CIRCLE (x, y), 1, 15            ' (draw in color 15 = white)
        CIRCLE (-x, y), 1, 15           ' (draw in color 15 = white)
        CIRCLE (fx, fy - .5), .5, 15
```

```
' save
    ox = x              ' save the current screen
    oy = y              ' variables (ox = old-x; oy = old-y)
    ofx = fx
    ofy = fy
    d = ((fx - x) ^ 2 + (fy - y) ^ 2) ^ .5
    PSET (frame, d), 15
    PSET (frame, y), 14
    frame = frame + .01
    FOR w = 1 TO 10000: NEXT w
LOOP
```

First Example—Running in Place

Now we'll place this flapping, swinging-ball thing above another periodic surface—a rippling pool of water (as seen in Figure 2-15). The script for this animation (BOLITA2.PI) is shown in the following listing.

```
// BOLITA2.PI
// Bumping, Flapping Line o' Balls over a Pool

start_frame 0
end_frame 179
total_frames 180
define index frame/total_frames

outfile balls

include "\PLY\COLORS.INC"

// set up background color & lights
background Navyblue
light <10, 10, -20>
light <-10, 10, -20>
light <0, 20, 0>

// set up the camera
```

continued on next page

Figure 2-15 Bolitas over water

continued from previous page

```
// ball 4

    if (phz > 0 && 4 > (5 - moving)) {
       define x4 8 * cos(ang * rad) + 4 * 2 - 6
       define y4 8 * sin(ang * rad) + 8
    }
    else {
       define x4 4 * 2 - 6
       define y4 0
    }

    if (phz < 0 && 4 < (moving + 1)) {
       define x4 8 * cos(ang * rad) + 4 * 2 - 6
       define y4 8 * sin(ang * rad) + 8
    }

// ball 5

    if (phz > 0 && 5 > (5 - moving)) {
       define x5 8 * cos(ang * rad) + 5 * 2 - 6
       define y5 8 * sin(ang * rad) + 8
    }
    else {
       define x5 5 * 2 - 6
       define y5 0
    }

    if (phz < 0 && 5 < (moving + 1)) {
       define x5 8 * cos(ang * rad) + 5 * 2 - 6
       define y5 8 * sin(ang * rad) + 8
    }

// make the mounts flap like a bird

    define phz2  10 * COS(2*t * rad) + exp(1.6 * (1 + cos((2*t - 80) * rad)))

    define ang2 45 + phz2

    define zm 8 * COS(ang2 * rad)
    define ym 8 * SIN(ang2 * rad) + 2
    define fy -4 * SIN(ang2 * rad) + 4

    define z 0

    define slateish
    texture {
       surface {
          ambient SlateBlue, 0.2
          diffuse SlateBlue, 0.6
          specular white, 0.6
          reflection white,0.5
          microfacet Reitz 10
          }
```

```
        }

    define real_dark <0.1,0.1,0.1>
    define onyx texture { metallic { color real_dark } }

    define blue_ripple
    texture {
        noise surface {
            color navyblue
            normal 2
            frequency 1
            phase -2*pi*t/360
            bump_scale 2
            ambient 0.2
            diffuse 0.4
            specular yellow, 0.5
            reflection 0.25
            microfacet Reitz 10
            }
    }


    define light_blue_ripple
    texture {
        noise surface {
            color navyblue
            normal 1
            frequency 1
            phase -2*pi*t/360
            bump_scale 0.2
            ambient 0.2
            diffuse 0.4
            specular yellow, 0.5
            reflection 0.25
            microfacet Reitz 10
            }
    }

// the flapping clacking contraption

    define bolita
        object {
            object { sphere <x1,y1+fy,z>,1 slateish }
          + object { sphere <x2,y2+fy,z>,1 slateish }
          + object { sphere <x3,y3+fy,z>,1 slateish }
          + object { sphere <x4,y4+fy,z>,1 slateish }
          + object { sphere <x5,y5+fy,z>,1 slateish }

    // the strings

          + object {cylinder <x1,y1+1+fy,z>,<1*2-6,ym,-zm>,0.05 shiny_orange }
          + object {cylinder <x2,y2+1+fy,z>,<2*2-6,ym,-zm>,0.05 shiny_orange }
          + object {cylinder <x3,y3+1+fy,z>,<3*2-6,ym,-zm>,0.05 shiny_orange }
```

continued on next page

75

continued from previous page

```
                + object {cylinder <x4,y4+1+fy,z>,<4*2-6,ym,-zm>,0.05 shiny_orange }
                + object {cylinder <x5,y5+1+fy,z>,<5*2-6,ym,-zm>,0.05 shiny_orange }

                + object { cylinder <x1,y1+1+fy,z>,<1*2-6,ym,zm>,0.05 shiny_orange }
                + object { cylinder <x2,y2+1+fy,z>,<2*2-6,ym,zm>,0.05 shiny_orange }
                + object { cylinder <x3,y3+1+fy,z>,<3*2-6,ym,zm>,0.05 shiny_orange }
                + object { cylinder <x4,y4+1+fy,z>,<4*2-6,ym,zm>,0.05 shiny_orange }
                + object { cylinder <x5,y5+1+fy,z>,<5*2-6,ym,zm>,0.05 shiny_orange }

        // the mounts

                + object { box <-6,ym-0.1,-zm-0.5>,<6,ym+0.5,-zm+0.5> onyx }
                + object { box <-6,ym-0.1, zm-0.5>,<6,ym+0.5, zm+0.5> onyx }
        }

        define copies fmod(frame,36)
        bolita { translate <-66+copies,0,0> }
        bolita { translate <-30+copies,0,0> }
        bolita { translate <  6+copies,0,0> }

// make watery walls
        object {
            object {cylinder <-100,0,0>,<100,0,0>,16}
          & object {box <-101,-8,-20>,<101,20,20>}
            rotate <125,0,0>
            translate <0,4,5>
            blue_ripple
        }

// reflecting pool
        object {
            polygon 4,<-100,-4,-10>,<-100,-4,10>,<100,-4,10>,<100,-4,-10>
            onyx
        }
```

A watery tunnel with a shiny floor was created by mapping our *blue_ripple* texture on a cylinder. Cutting the side out of it allows the camera to see inside. The shiny floor was added to clean up the edge of the cylinder and double the apparent number of objects moving in the scene.

Comments

It's possible to continue adding more and more periodic motions all linked to the basic motions we've created. Rather than a constant forward linear motion, we could make this motion surge and glide. We could make the entire frame swoop up and down, simulating the real motions of birds as they flap their wings. We could periodically halt the flapping or change its rate. We just keep nesting the motions.

2.4 How do I...
Create a five-dimensional dripping faucet?

You'll find the code for this in: PLY\CHAPTER2\DRIP

Problem

Creating convincing animations of fluids in motion cannot be done with conventional geometric primitives like spheres and cylinders. Polyray supports a variety of tear-drop shaped objects whose outer surfaces are defined by some polynomial equation (check out PIRIFORM.PI and TEAR5.PI in the POLY directory), and it might be possible through careful selection of coefficients to produce a dripping faucet animation with a couple of them. However, an easier way to do this is to use a primitive known as a *blob*, which acts much as its name suggests. It's so useful for generating really interesting animations that we're devoting an entire chapter to it later on (Chapter 7). As an introduction, our simple dripping faucet animation shows off what a blob is capable of and how to use it.

Technique

Try to humor me on this one, OK? A dripping faucet in three dimensions has a drop moving down a single axis. By extension, a 4-D dripping faucet would drip simultaneously down two perpendicular axes, and a 5-D faucet would drip down three perpendicular axes. If we can imagine three orthogonal gravity fields, let's mirror them, and cause our drops to go in six different directions at the same time, namely down both positive and negative Cartesian axes. Droplets form out of a central transparent ball and exit in six different directions simultaneously.

This animation exploits the fact that metaballs (the things blobs are made of) can hide inside each other and that when two metaballs move apart, they can form little football shapes and then disappear altogether. Figure 2-17 shows a series of blobs comprised of two metaballs. The metaballs have a maximum interaction distance set at 1.0. At this distance of 1.0, they're footballing, and by 1.1, they're gone.

Steps

5DRIP.PI starts with three metaballs per axis, for a total of 18, spaced one unit apart (Figure 2-18), and makes them all move away from the origin by multiplying their distance from the origin by a linearly increasing factor

continued from previous page

```
0.1, 3.0, <-1, 1, 0>*framer,
0.1, 3.0, < 0,-1, 1>*framer,
0.1, 3.0, <-1, 0, 1>*framer,

0.1, 3.0, < 1,-1, 0>*framer,
0.1, 3.0, < 0, 1,-1>*framer,
0.1, 3.0, < 1, 0,-1>*framer,

0.1, 3.0, < 1, 1, 1>*framer,
0.1, 3.0, <-1,-1,-1>*framer,
0.1, 3.0, <-1, 1, 1>*framer,
0.1, 3.0, < 1,-1, 1>*framer,
0.1, 3.0, < 1, 1,-1>*framer,
0.1, 3.0, <-1, 1,-1>*framer,
0.1, 3.0, < 1,-1,-1>*framer,
0.1, 3.0, <-1,-1, 1>*framer,

0.1, 3.0, < 2, 2, 0>*framer,
0.1, 3.0, < 0, 2, 2>*framer,
0.1, 3.0, < 2, 0, 2>*framer,

0.1, 3.0, <-2,-2, 0>*framer,
0.1, 3.0, < 0,-2,-2>*framer,
0.1, 3.0, <-2, 0,-2>*framer,

0.1, 3.0, <-2, 2, 0>*framer,
0.1, 3.0, < 0,-2, 2>*framer,
0.1, 3.0, <-2, 0, 2>*framer,

0.1, 3.0, < 2,-2, 0>*framer,
0.1, 3.0, < 0, 2,-2>*framer,
0.1, 3.0, < 2, 0,-2>*framer,

0.1, 3.0, < 2, 2, 2>*framer,
0.1, 3.0, <-2,-2,-2>*framer,
0.1, 3.0, <-2, 2, 2>*framer,
0.1, 3.0, < 2,-2, 2>*framer,
0.1, 3.0, < 2, 2,-2>*framer,
0.1, 3.0, <-2, 2,-2>*framer,
0.1, 3.0, < 2,-2,-2>*framer,
0.1, 3.0, <-2,-2, 2>*framer,

0.1, 3.0, < 3, 3, 0>*framer,
0.1, 3.0, < 0, 3, 3>*framer,
0.1, 3.0, < 3, 0, 3>*framer,

0.1, 3.0, <-3,-3, 0>*framer,
0.1, 3.0, < 0,-3,-3>*framer,
0.1, 3.0, <-3, 0,-3>*framer,

0.1, 3.0, <-3, 3, 0>*framer,
0.1, 3.0, < 0,-3, 3>*framer,
```

```
    0.1, 3.0, <-3, 0, 3>*framer,

    0.1, 3.0, < 3,-3, 0>*framer,
    0.1, 3.0, < 0, 3,-3>*framer,
    0.1, 3.0, < 3, 0,-3>*framer,

    0.1, 3.0, < 3, 3, 3>*framer,
    0.1, 3.0, <-3,-3,-3>*framer,
    0.1, 3.0, <-3, 3, 3>*framer,
    0.1, 3.0, < 3,-3, 3>*framer,
    0.1, 3.0, < 3, 3,-3>*framer,
    0.1, 3.0, <-3, 3,-3>*framer,
    0.1, 3.0, < 3,-3,-3>*framer,
    0.1, 3.0, <-3,-3, 3>*framer,

    0.5, 3.0, <0,0,0>
  root_solver Ferrari
  u_steps 20
  v_steps 20
  blue_glass
  }

dripper { rotate <0,frame,0> }

define shift frame/30

if (fmod(frame,2)==0)
   ground1 { translate <-2*shift,0,2*shift> }
else
   ground2 { translate <-2*shift,0,2*shift> }
```

As was previously mentioned, two alternative ground planes, *ground1* and *ground2,* are defined with patterns that are exact opposites; where one is black, the other is white. They'd actually be photographic negatives of each other. Depending on whether the frame counter is odd or even, one of these two grounds gets called. Alternating the grounds generates a sense (positive or negative) on the checkerboard background, giving us a flickering background.

Since the dripper blob is so detailed (60 blobs rather than 18), we decided to rotate it while it was evolving to afford a better view of the structure. It does a quarter turn during the 90 frames of this animation.

Comments

The more objects used to define a blob, the longer it takes to render, all else being equal. Refraction takes longer to render than reflection, so in developing fluid animations of your own, you might try a nontransparent texture first.

2.5 How do I...

Generate a complex surface without resorting to complex triangle grids?

You'll find the code for this in: PLY\CHAPTER2\TILE

Problem

The usual way to define a complex surface like a face or a mountain range is to define a whole lot of little triangles that approximate the surface in a mosaic fashion. This takes a large data file and some expensive digitization equipment. Many vendors sell remarkably detailed 3-D models based on collections of triangles or polygons that define cows and shoes and airplanes and cities. You can probably find whatever you're looking for in some catalog, but be prepared to spend some money.

In contrast, heightfields are remarkably simple ways to get incredibly complex surfaces from fairly simple equations without having to resort to a triangle mesh. Well, you *personally* don't have to resort to them—the ray tracer generates triangles that it uses internally, so they become its problem, not yours.

Technique

In Section 2.1, we used a heightfield for the terrain. We'll use another one here, one with shifting walls and alternating patches of smooth (slowly varying) and noisy (rapidly varying) heights. It's based on raising the height of a point on a surface by an exponent generated by dividing the cosine of its x location by the sine of its z location. For those of you having problems visualizing this, it's shown in Figure 2-21.

Figure 2-21 A surface defined by $x^{(\cos(x)/\sin(z))} + z^{(\sin(x)/\cos(z))}$ overlaid by grid

At certain points, the surface easily extends well beyond the next galaxy, so we make use of *fmods* (floating point modulus... remainder after division by some arbitrary number) to yank it back onto our monitor. We also scale the height of the surface so that it rises and falls like the surface of the sea. To heighten the sense of rising and falling, we'll add a stable grid of spheres that will act like a pier in this sea. These spheres are placed at 50% of the maximum height of the sea, which allows us to see how much the surface as a whole is moving up and down. We start by staring at a small region on the surface, then graduate to a flyover.

Steps

This first animation (TILE1.PI) focuses in on a single region on the surface. The camera is controlled by a tricornered function (a deltoid) centered on a square where a reasonably interesting surface evolution was found during some test renders. The grid size of the heightfield, which determines how many triangles are laid down, is made to vary from frame to frame, resulting in changes in spatial resolution and shifting features. The height is accented by a 3-D yellow and blue checker function. It's been scaled and positioned to hide the fact that it's a checker. Checkers are overused textures in ray traced images and should be avoided whenever possible. A grid function lays down some lines of spheres marking borders between smooth and noisy areas, and giving a better reference to the large scale height shifts in the smoother areas on the heightfield.

```
// TILE1.PI
// Heightfield Tiled Function
// Polyray input file: Jeff Bowermaster

start_frame 0
end_frame   359
total_frames 360
OUTFILE TILE1
define angle_nor frame/total_frames

define pi 3.14159
define pi2 2*pi
define rad pi/180

define a 2
define b 0.5
define phz1 0
define phz2 0.25

define sides 3-1

// two Deltoids
```

continued on next page

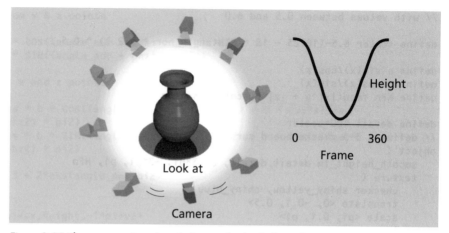

Figure 2-22 The camera motion, what it looks at, and its height during the animation

```
define a sin(x)/cos(z)
define b cos(z)/sin(x)
define HFn fmod(|x|^a + |z|^b,scaler)/scaler
```

is odd, but it has some periodicity with respect to pi. This periodicity is exploited to hide the checkerboard nature of the texture map, which we apply to color the surface different colors at different heights, and to give the map a pseudo-topographic look.

The final element in the image is a gridded object, our reference plane, which is generated by reading a targa file and putting a colored sphere into our image wherever a pixel of the same color exists in the targa image (Figure 2-23). We could have just generated an include file full of spheres in

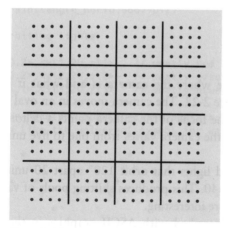

Figure 2-23 GRIDMASK.TGA, the gridded reference map for our graph paper in the image

the appropriate places, but this kind of graph paper reference grid is exactly what gridded objects are good at, and learning something new about Polyray is always worthwhile.

TILE.PI is a bit tough to watch for any length of time, because it rocks and surges quite a bit. Though really just a simple oval flyby, TILE.PI creates a more pleasing animation by eliminating spatial resolution shifts and moving close to the surface.

```
// TILE2.PI
// Heightfield Tiled Function
// Polyray input file: Jeff Bowermaster

start_frame 0
end_frame   359
total_frames 360

outfile "tile2"

define angle_nor frame/total_frames

define pi 3.14159
define pi2 2*pi
define rad pi/180

define a 2
define b 0.5
define phz1 0
define phz2 0.25

define sides 3-1

define vx pi  * COS((angle_nor + phz1) * pi2)
define vz pi2 * SIN((angle_nor + phz1) * pi2)

define lx sides * b * COS((angle_nor + phz2) * pi2) + b * COS(sides * (angle_nor + phz2) * pi2)
define lz sides * b * SIN((angle_nor + phz2) * pi2) - b * SIN(sides * (angle_nor + phz2) * pi2)

define height 3 + 2*cos(angle_nor*pi2)

viewpoint {
   from <1.5*pi+vx,height,-1*pi+vz>
   at <1.5*pi+lx,0,-1*pi+lz>
   up <0,1,0>
   angle 30
   resolution 320,200
   aspect 1.43
   }

include "\PLY\COLORS.INC"

// position the lights on a circle radius 40 that rotates once
```

continued on next page

continued from previous page

```
define xl1 40*cos(angle_nor*pi2)
define zl1 40*sin(angle_nor*pi2)

define xl2 40*cos((angle_nor+0.333)*pi2)
define zl2 40*sin((angle_nor+0.333)*pi2)

define xl3 40*cos((angle_nor+0.666)*pi2)
define zl3 40*sin((angle_nor+0.666)*pi2)

light <1,0.4,0.2>,<xl1,20,zl1>     // tricolor orbiting lights
light <0.4,1,0.2>,<xl2,20,zl2>
light <0.2,0.4,1>,<xl3,20,zl3>

define scaler 6.5-(18.25 - 18 * SIN(angle_nor * pi2 )) ^ 0.5


define a sin(x)/cos(z)
define b cos(z)/sin(x)
define HFn fmod(|x|^a + |z|^b,scaler)/scaler

define detail 250
// define a 3-D checkerboard surface
object {
    smooth_height_fn detail,detail, 0, 3*pi, -3*pi, pi, HFn
    texture {
       checker shiny_yellow, shiny_blue
       translate <0, -0.1, 0.5>
       scale <pi, 0.1, pi>
       }
    }

// lay down a grid of spheres to pick reasonable fly points

// make an array of fiducial spheres

define ball1 object { sphere <0.0, 0.0, 0.0>, 1 shiny_blue}
define ball2 object { sphere <0.0, 0.0, 0.0>, 1 shiny_coral}
define ball3 object { sphere <0.0, 0.0, 0.0>, 1 mirror}

define snf pi/25

object {
    gridded "gridmask.tga",
       ball1
       ball2
       ball3
    translate <-50, 0, -50>
    scale <snf, snf, snf>
    translate <pi2, 0.5, -pi2>
    }
```

 2.6 How do I...
Generate tumbling motions?

You'll find the code for this in: PLY\CHAPTER2\DICE

Problem

Examining an object from all sides isn't as easy as it sounds. Constant rotations about an axis, besides being rather plain, don't bring every side of an object into view. And constant rotation about several axes just adds together to create a simple rotation about a composite axis. So the trick here (surprise, surprise) is *not* to use constant rotations, but to vary the rotational speed and phase about several axes, and some combination will eventually make every side of an object come around to the front. One type of motion that fits the bill is the stitch pattern on a baseball.

Technique

What would you do if someone handed you a diamond, I mean a really HUGE diamond? You'd run away with it, of course (silly question). No, no no, let's say there are guards with guns and poor social skills staring at you with beady little eyes below protruding foreheads. OK, you'll just have to be satisfied with looking at it. What would you do then; would you hold it at arm's length and just stare at from one angle? Of course not! You'd tumble it end over end, upside down, right side up, inside out (tough, by the way), backwards, forwards, you'd try to look at that thing from every conceivable angle. Fine. You get the idea. That's just what we're going to try to do right now.

   In order to demonstrate that this motion indeed fits the bill, bringing all sides into view without bias, we approach it analytically. Figure 2-24 shows in patented crypto-form (no labels on any axis) the *x, y,* and *z* angular displacements, the sum of the distances of each vertex from its original orientation (used to find loop points), histograms (sums as bar charts) of the number of frames each corner and each face spends in the foreground (there's a difference), and the cube as it tumbles. The goal here is to find a set of motions that generates flat histograms for the faces or corners, meaning that all faces or corners spend about the same amount of time in the foreground. The tumbling equations that produced this result are

$$xrotate = factor * (2 * SIN(ang) + SIN(3 * ang) / 3)$$
$$yrotate = factor * (2 * COS(ang) - COS(3 * ang) / 3)$$
$$zrotate = factor * (COS(2 * ang))$$

These cover a range for *any* of 0 to 360.

continued from previous page

```
//define vz SIN(ang3)

viewpoint {
   from <vx, vy, vz> * 8
   at <0,0,0>
   up <0,1,0>
   angle 40
   resolution 160,100
   aspect 1.433
   }
background SkyBlue

include "\PLY\COLORS.INC"
spot_light  white,  <-2+vx,vy,vz>*8,<0,0,0>,3,5,20
spot_light  white,  < 2+vx,vy,vz>*8,<0,0,0>,3,5,20

define die1
   object {
      object {box <-2,-2,-2>,<2,2,2> matte_white}
   //1
    - object {sphere < 0, 0,-2>, 0.4 matte_black }
   //2
    - object {sphere <-2,-1,-1>, 0.4 matte_black }
    - object {sphere <-2, 1, 1>, 0.4 matte_black }
   //3
    - object {sphere <-1,-2,-1>, 0.4 matte_black }
    - object {sphere < 0,-2, 0>, 0.4 matte_black }
    - object {sphere < 1,-2, 1>, 0.4 matte_black }
   //4
    - object {sphere <-1, 2,-1>, 0.4 matte_black }
    - object {sphere < 1, 2,-1>, 0.4 matte_black }
    - object {sphere <-1, 2, 1>, 0.4 matte_black }
    - object {sphere < 1, 2, 1>, 0.4 matte_black }
   //5
    - object {sphere < 2, 0, 0>, 0.4 matte_black }
    - object {sphere < 2,-1,-1>, 0.4 matte_black }
    - object {sphere < 2, 1, 1>, 0.4 matte_black }
    - object {sphere < 2,-1, 1>, 0.4 matte_black }
    - object {sphere < 2, 1,-1>, 0.4 matte_black }
   //6
    - object {sphere <-1, 1, 2>, 0.4 matte_black }
    - object {sphere < 0, 1, 2>, 0.4 matte_black }
    - object {sphere < 1, 1, 2>, 0.4 matte_black }
    - object {sphere <-1,-1, 2>, 0.4 matte_black }
    - object {sphere < 0,-1, 2>, 0.4 matte_black }
    - object {sphere < 1,-1, 2>, 0.4 matte_black }
}

define dice
object {
   die1
```

```
* object { sphere < 0, 0, 0>, 2.85 matte_white}
}

dice
```

For less snap, the second term can be omitted from the *vx, vy,* and *vz* equations, and the results (commented out in DICE3.PI) produce a simple orbital motion, tilted 45° to all three axes. When there is little else in your scene besides the one object, zooming the camera around the object is just as effective as holding the camera steady and tumbling the object. Some frames from DICE3.PI are shown in Figure 2-28.

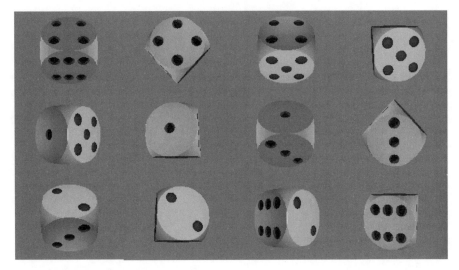

Figure 2-28 Frames from DICE3.PI

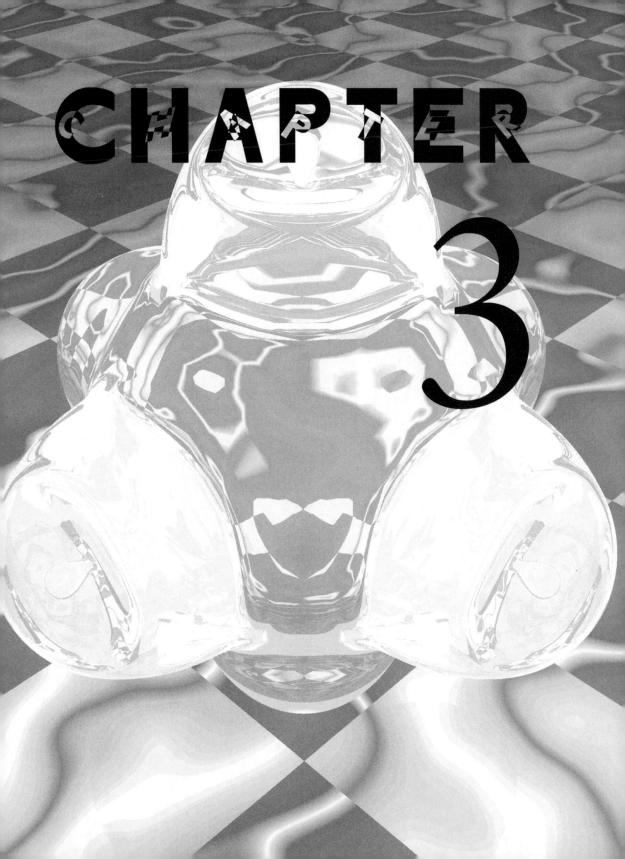

CHAPTER

3

3

POINTS OF VIEW

As is true with most things, perception depends on your point of view. In this chapter, we'll show animations where we either shift the point of view to reveal some hidden facet of an image, or create an image that is not what it seems. Shifting around off-camera elements—for example, random wandering shapes intersecting colored spotlights at various levels—can produce unusual textures that would be hard to generate on the objects themselves. Camera motions can transform flat, 2-D images into dramatic 3-D environments that pull the viewer right into the screen. The underlying theme here is that clever tricks can make complex scenes from simple data files, and that moving around really adds reality to the spatial feel of animations.

3.1 How do I...
Create a dazzling background with moving bands of color?

You'll find the code for this in: PLY\CHAPTER3\BARCODE

Problem

Let's say you need a vibrant background with randomly shifting color bands. Polyray has a "noise" surface texture with several linear color mapping functions that would work. We'll cover those in the next section. Generating randomly changing color maps to feed these textures could be a real chore. As an alternative, we'll use colored lights filtered through shifting off-camera elements to generate the same effect with less work.

Technique

In the main library of North Carolina State University, there was (and might still be) an interesting sculpture where a series of slats mounted a short distance from a wall were illuminated by an array of blinking colored lights. The lights were sequenced in a semi-random fashion, and formed a giant, dynamic Technicolor bar code on the wall. The colored patches were a combination of both the lights themselves and the complementary colors formed as a result of the way eyes deal with the shadows of colored lights. It's really easy to model this with a ray tracer.

Writing the Program

This animation requires separate controls for a great number of objects. Rather than come up with separate functions to control each element, we'll use a sine function and space our variables out along this single function.

In Figure 3-1, there are 11 spotlights pointing towards a wall with an equal number of cylinders (seen end-on) intersecting their light from behind a camera. Each spot has its own color. Some oscillating spheres traveling across the scene are added and made shiny to show off what's going on behind the scenes. The camera points at the wall and can't see what the cylinders are doing. From this perspective, we'll move the spots left and right, the cylinders left and right, and the oscillating spheres top to bottom.

Everything shifts: the position of the lights, their intensity, the size of the oscillating spheres, the positions of the blocking cylinders. All is done with a *sine* function indexed to the normalized frame count (*frame/total_frames*). This makes the animation smoothly loop at the end, as shown in BARCODE.PI—the next listing.

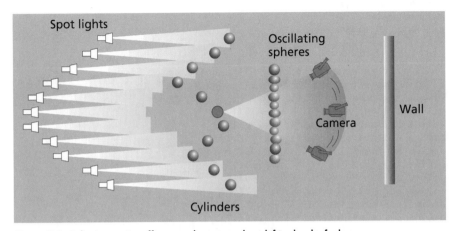

Figure 3-1 Lights intersecting off-camera elements produce shifting bands of color

```
//BARCODE.PI  - Colored Lights and Tubes

start_frame 0
end_frame 59
total_frames 60

outfile "barc"

include "\PLY\COLORS.INC"

viewpoint {
   from <0,0,1>
   at <0,0,5>
   up <0,1,0>
   angle 45
   resolution 320,200
   aspect 1.43
   }

background MidnightBlue

// 11 different colors

define c01 <1.000,0.500,0.000>        //coral
define c02 <0.500,0.500,0.000>        //yellow
define c03 <1.000,0.000,0.500>        //red purple
define c04 <0.500,0.000,1.000>        //blue violet
define c05 <0.000,1.000,0.500>        //green blue
define c06 <0.000,0.500,1.000>        //blue green
define c07 <1.000,0.000,0.000>        //red
define c08 <1.000,0.250,0.000>        //orange
define c09 <0.000,0.000,1.000>        //blue
define c10 <1.000,0.000,1.000>        //magenta
define c11 <0.000,0.250,1.000>        //aqua
```

continued on next page

continued from previous page

```
define amp 2
define pi 3.14159
define index frame/total_frames

// 11 factors equally spaced 1/11th units apart in phase space
// with amp set at 2, these will range from -2 to 2

define a01 amp*sin(2*pi*(index+1/11))
define a02 amp*sin(2*pi*(index+2/11))
define a03 amp*sin(2*pi*(index+3/11))
define a04 amp*sin(2*pi*(index+4/11))
define a05 amp*sin(2*pi*(index+5/11))
define a06 amp*sin(2*pi*(index+6/11))
define a07 amp*sin(2*pi*(index+7/11))
define a08 amp*sin(2*pi*(index+8/11))
define a09 amp*sin(2*pi*(index+9/11))
define a10 amp*sin(2*pi*(index+10/11))
define a11 amp*sin(2*pi*(index+11/11))

// these will go from 0 to 2
define b01 (a01+amp)/amp
define b02 (a02+amp)/amp
define b03 (a03+amp)/amp
define b04 (a04+amp)/amp
define b05 (a05+amp)/amp
define b06 (a06+amp)/amp
define b07 (a07+amp)/amp
define b08 (a08+amp)/amp
define b09 (a09+amp)/amp
define b10 (a10+amp)/amp
define b11 (a11+amp)/amp

// use the factors above, but make them go from 0 to 2

// dim lets us simultaneously reduces all the lights
// multiple lights usually overexpose RT scenes

define dim 0.5

// 11 colored spot_lights, pointing along the z-axis.  Their
// distance from the wall changes from -8 to -12, and varies
// in brightness from double their nominal brightness to off

define dist -10  // how far back the spots are
define strt 5    // inner angle for spotlight
define fini 10   // outer angle ""

// these are the lower lights (y = -2.8)
spot_light c01*dim*b08,<-5,-2.8,dist+a01>,<-5,-2.8,0>,3,strt,fini
spot_light c02*dim*b05,<-4,-2.8,dist+a02>,<-4,-2.8,0>,3,strt,fini
spot_light c03*dim*b01,<-3,-2.8,dist+a03>,<-3,-2.8,0>,3,strt,fini
spot_light c04*dim*b03,<-2,-2.8,dist+a04>,<-2,-2.8,0>,3,strt,fini
```

```
spot_light c05*dim*b11,<-1,-2.8,dist+a05>,<-1,-2.8,0>,3,strt,fini
spot_light c06*dim*b02,< 0,-2.8,dist+a06>,< 0,-2.8,0>,3,strt,fini
spot_light c07*dim*b10,< 1,-2.8,dist+a07>,< 1,-2.8,0>,3,strt,fini
spot_light c08*dim*b04,< 2,-2.8,dist+a08>,< 2,-2.8,0>,3,strt,fini
spot_light c09*dim*b09,< 3,-2.8,dist+a09>,< 3,-2.8,0>,3,strt,fini
spot_light c10*dim*b06,< 4,-2.8,dist+a10>,< 4,-2.8,0>,3,strt,fini
spot_light c11*dim*b07,< 5,-2.8,dist+a11>,< 5,-2.8,0>,3,strt,fini

// these are the upper lights (y = 2.8)
spot_light c01*dim*b08,<-5,2.8,dist+a01>,<-5,2.8,0>,3,strt,fini
spot_light c02*dim*b05,<-4,2.8,dist+a02>,<-4,2.8,0>,3,strt,fini
spot_light c03*dim*b01,<-3,2.8,dist+a03>,<-3,2.8,0>,3,strt,fini
spot_light c04*dim*b03,<-2,2.8,dist+a04>,<-2,2.8,0>,3,strt,fini
spot_light c05*dim*b11,<-1,2.8,dist+a05>,<-1,2.8,0>,3,strt,fini
spot_light c06*dim*b02,< 0,2.8,dist+a06>,< 0,2.8,0>,3,strt,fini
spot_light c07*dim*b10,< 1,2.8,dist+a07>,< 1,2.8,0>,3,strt,fini
spot_light c08*dim*b04,< 2,2.8,dist+a08>,< 2,2.8,0>,3,strt,fini
spot_light c09*dim*b09,< 3,2.8,dist+a09>,< 3,2.8,0>,3,strt,fini
spot_light c10*dim*b06,< 4,2.8,dist+a10>,< 4,2.8,0>,3,strt,fini
spot_light c11*dim*b07,< 5,2.8,dist+a11>,< 5,2.8,0>,3,strt,fini


// The intersecting cylinders we use to create the shadows
object { cylinder <-5,-5,0>,<-5,5,0+a01/2>,0.25 matte_white }
object { cylinder <-4,-5,0>,<-4,5,0+a03/2>,0.25 matte_white }
object { cylinder <-3,-5,0>,<-3,5,0+a05/2>,0.25 matte_white }
object { cylinder <-2,-5,0>,<-2,5,0+a07/2>,0.25 matte_white }
object { cylinder <-1,-5,0>,<-1,5,0+a09/2>,0.25 matte_white }
object { cylinder <-0,-5,0>,< 0,5,0+a10/2>,0.25 matte_white }
object { cylinder < 1,-5,0>,< 1,5,0+a02/2>,0.25 matte_white }
object { cylinder < 2,-5,0>,< 2,5,0+a04/2>,0.25 matte_white }
object { cylinder < 3,-5,0>,< 3,5,0+a06/2>,0.25 matte_white }
object { cylinder < 4,-5,0>,< 4,5,0+a08/2>,0.25 matte_white }
object { cylinder < 5,-5,0>,< 5,5,0+a11/2>,0.25 matte_white }

// our wall (a big disc, the edges don't show)
object {disc <0,0,15>,<0,0,1>,10 matte_white }

// prepare a texture to reflect the scene on spheres
define mirror2
texture {
   surface {
      ambient white, -0.5
      diffuse white, 0.5
      specular 0
      reflection white*2, 2
      }
   }

// make alternating growing and shrinking functions
// at 3 times the normal loop rate.  Kissing spheres;
// squeeze1+squeeze2 = 0.5, the sphere spacing
```

continued on next page

continued from previous page

```
define squeeze1 0.25 + 0.05*sin(6*pi*index)
define squeeze2 0.25 - 0.05*sin(6*pi*index)

// 11 mirrored spheres to hide the spot_light overlap and
// show us what's going on behind the camera.
// "index"ing the x position variable makes the spheres
// travel right.

object {sphere <index-2.5,0,3>,squeeze1 mirror2 }
object {sphere <index-2.0,0,3>,squeeze2 mirror2 }
object {sphere <index-1.5,0,3>,squeeze1 mirror2 }
object {sphere <index-1.0,0,3>,squeeze2 mirror2 }
object {sphere <index-0.5,0,3>,squeeze1 mirror2 }
object {sphere <index+0.0,0,3>,squeeze2 mirror2 }
object {sphere <index+0.5,0,3>,squeeze1 mirror2 }
object {sphere <index+1.0,0,3>,squeeze2 mirror2 }
object {sphere <index+1.5,0,3>,squeeze1 mirror2 }
object {sphere <index+2.0,0,3>,squeeze2 mirror2 }
object {sphere <index+2.5,0,3>,squeeze1 mirror2 }
```

Steps

Here are the steps you need to follow to render and view this animation:

1. Change to the PLY\CHAPTER3\BARCODE directory.
2. Type PR BARCODE.
3. After 60 images render, type DTA barc* /0barc /s3 /c4.
4. View the flic with AAPLAYHI.

How It Works

The vectors *c01-c11* define 11 different colors in RGB (red/green/blue) color specifications. They're mainly saturated colors (rather than pastels), needed to make distinct bright bands on the wall.

The variables *a01-a11* are 11 factors equally spaced along the length of a sine wave. The variable *amp* sets the gain so that these variables go from -2 to 2. We'll use these to shift the positions of the spotlights back and forth.

The variables *b01-b11* are derived from *a01-a11,* but range from 0 to 2 to control the intensity of the lights.

Two rows of spotlights are defined, but rather than sequentially applying our position and light intensity factors to them, we scramble the variables to prevent the lights from coming on in waves.

The array of cylinders to intersect our lights is positioned along the plane where *z = 0*, and these cylinders are shifted plus or minus one unit about this plane during the animation.

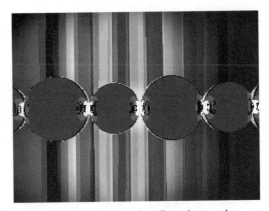

Figure 3-2 Colored bands with oscillating kissing spheres

A wall for the lights and shadows to fall on is created using a disc. A line of kissing mirrored spheres is generated to reflect the cylinders behind the camera, and a 60 frame animation is created. A sample of the output is shown in Figure 3-2.

Variations

You might try substituting some evolving geometric shape for the spheres, flex the disk or wrinkle it periodically, or place the lights on a conveyor belt like a treadmill and make all the colors and shapes warp in a more complex twisted fashion. This is one of those animations where you can just keep shoveling it in. Adding a collection of spiraling, orbital transparent spheres would be fun, because the colored bands would bend and blend inside them, but be aware that refraction takes much more time to render.

3.2 How do I...
Modify the texture of an object synchronized with the camera motion?

You'll find the code for this in: PLY\CHAPTER3\ROCKY

Problem

A viewpoint swaying back and forth in the trailing edges of a comet, spewing multihued gases would involve quite an elaborate particle systems animation and some fairly novel 3-D texturing scheme for the particles. But you can easily get a similar effect by viewing a shifting texture mapped on a sphere with a wide angle lens.

Technique

This animation is not difficult to produce, but the effects are difficult to watch. It's the insides of a sphere with a noise surface texture mapped on it, and we shift the phase of the color map and vary its turbulence as we rock it back and forth. Dramamine is highly recommended.

Noise Surface Textures

A few words on noise surfaces textures are appropriate at this point. Examine the rainbow texture in the following Polyray data file RAINBOW.PI.

```
// RAINBOW.PI

viewpoint {
    from <10,10,-10>
    up    <0, 1, 0>
    at    <0,-3,0>
    angle 40
    resolution 320,240
    aspect 1.333
    }


light <1,1,1>,<-20,10,0>
light <1,1,1>,< 20,10,0>

background midnightblue

define rainbow
texture {
    noise surface {
        position_fn 5
        lookup_fn 1
        octaves 1
        turbulence 2
        ambient 0.2
        diffuse 0.8
        color_map(
        [0.00, 0.16, red, orange ]
        [0.16, 0.33, orange, yellow ]
        [0.33, 0.48, yellow, green ]
        [0.48, 0.67, green, blue ]
        [0.67, 0.83, blue, violet ]
        [0.83, 1.00, violet, black ])
    }
}

object {
    polygon 4, <-6,-1, -6>, <-6,-1,  6>,
               < 6,-1,  6>, < 6,-1, -6>
    rainbow
    }
```

The noise surface function generates a number between 0 and 1 for every point in 3-D space. These aren't exactly regular, but they're not completely random either. They vary slowly and smoothly over short distances, but appear random over longer ones. The mapping of these variations on an object and the way they vary are controlled by built-in Polyray *position_fn* and *lookup_fn* functions. You select a number for the effect you want and Polyray handles the details. The values *5* and *1,* used here for *position_fn* and *lookup_fn,* specify varying the color map according to the distance around the *y* axis using a sawtooth function. Linear, spherical, and sine variations are also available. Check out the text listing just above the *color_phase* texture defined in ROCK1.PI (following) or look in the Polyray documentation for more details. Octaves and turbulence control the rate of change of the colors.

The *color_map* gives the relationship between the value returned by the noise function and its color. The first number in the color map specifies the start of the zone, the second the end, and the two colors after that the colors at both ends of a range. Colors in between are interpolated from the values at both ends. A value of *0.0* returns red, *0.08* (the midpoint of the first range) gives a color halfway between red and orange, *0.33* returns yellow and so on throughout the rainbow we've defined.

The shifting colors we're after are achieved by phasing the intensities of colors in a simple (but lengthy) *color_map.* The intensities of the 30 colors we create (each phased 12° apart for a total of 360°) vary sinusoidally across this *color_map* (see Figure 3-3). Holding red fixed, green is shifted left so that after 30 frames it's back where it started. Blue is shifted the same way, only at twice the speed of green. Somewhere around frame 23, the intensities of all three colors line up, which produces a black and white color map. The

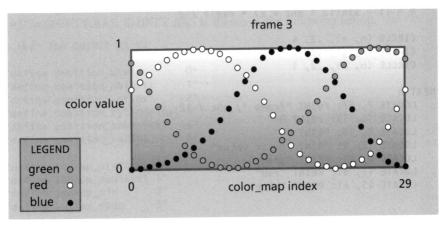

Figure 3-3 Phased intensities of red, green, and blue for 30 colors

continued from previous page

```
        diffuse 0.8
        specular 0.3
        microfacet Reitz 5
        color_map(
        [0.000, 0.033, <a00, b00, c00>, <a01, b01, c01> ]
        [0.033, 0.067, <a01, b01, c01>, <a02, b02, c02> ]
        [0.067, 0.100, <a02, b02, c02>, <a03, b03, c03> ]
        ...

        [0.933, 0.967, <a28, b28, c28>, <a29, b29, c29> ]
        [0.967, 1.000, <a29, b29, c29>, <a00, b00, c00> ])
            }
    scale <100,100,100>
}

define tx 100*sin(phz*rad)
define ty 50*sin(phz*rad)
define tz 100*sin(phz*rad)

// Create a volume
object {
    sphere <0,0,0>, 540
    color_phase
    translate <tx,ty,tz>
    }
```

ROCK1.PI was generated manually by pasting together the outputs of COLORMAP.BAS and SHIFTY.BAS, creating a main file which defined the camera, light, output files, and objects. The same thing could have been done including those outputs in the main file by using "include" commands, as shown in the following example, ROCK2.PI.

```
// ROCK2.PI - Rocking color weirdness, done with include files

start_frame 0
end_frame 29
total_frames 30

outfile "roc"

define pi 3.1415927
define rad pi/180

define phz 360*frame/total_frames

// Lights

light <0.5, 0.5, 0.5>, < 180, 150, -150>
light <0.5, 0.5, 0.5>, < 0, 100, -15>
light <0.5, 0.5, 0.5>, < 0, 0, 0>

// Camera
```

```
viewpoint {
   from <300,200,-250>
   at <0,0,0>
   up <0,1,0>
   angle 120
   aspect 1.433
   resolution 320,200
   }

// Action
include "colormap.inc"

include "text1.inc"

define tx 100*sin(phz*rad)
define ty 50*sin(phz*rad)
define tz 100*sin(phz*rad)

// Create a volume
object {
   sphere <0,0,0>, 540
   color_phase
   translate <tx,ty,tz>
   }
```

Both ROCK1.PI and ROCK2.PI generate 30 frames that resemble Figure 3-4, except they sway.

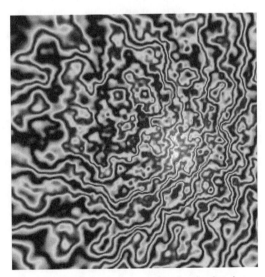

Figure 3-4 A wiggly streaming texture that develops during our animation

How It Works

This animation works by shifting the phase of the red, green, and blue portions of a series of colors to produce shifting periodic color bands. The motivator needs to be a phase angle varying from 0 to 360° over the course of the total frame count, which in this case is 30. The variable *phz*, defined as

```
define phz 360*frame/total_frames
```

fills the bill. The variables *a00-a29, b00-b29* and *c00-c29* specify the red, green, and blue portions of our color map. Note that in the script

```
define a00 (1 + sin(  6 * rad)) / 2
define b00 (1 + cos((phz +   6) * rad)) / 2
define c00 (1 - sin((2*phz +   6) * rad)) / 2
```

a00—the red intensity—doesn't depend on *phz*, making it fixed throughout the animation. Green varies by *phz*, and blue by twice that (*2*phz*). We generate 30 colors that span the spectrum by adding a 12° offset to each successive color.

We used defines to convert meaningless numbers into a text description of the available mapping functions. While the numbers would have worked just as well, the text is far more informative. A noise surface is defined, where we vary the turbulence between *1* and *2* during the animation to stir things up a bit:

```
turbulence 1.5+0.5*sin(phz*rad)
```

The long *color_map* listing—which uses the colors defined in the previous section—is compiled and scaled up 100 times until it is the right size for the 540-unit sphere we're mapping it onto. Phased translations for the texture as *tx, ty, tz* are generated, rocking the texture back and forth sinusoidally on the sphere. Once the sphere is completed, map the texture onto it, and shift that texture around.

Comments

There are an endless number of variations on this simple animation. Experiment with the various texture mapping functions and turbulence values, shift the colors of the lights, vary the bumpiness of the texture or create a whole series of spheres and fly through them.

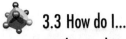

3.3 How do I...
Produce a disco inferno?

You'll find the code for this in: PLY\CHAPTER3\NTCLUB

Problem

Lights! Tables! Loud music! Alien cubes from the 4th dimension! No, wait, that wasn't supposed to be there... Of course it was! This is night life! Dance clubs are designed to overload the sensory inputs of both the eyes and the ears, with little regard for style or taste. The louder the music, the brighter the colors, the greater the number of frantically panning spotlights, the better. This sounds like a job for an amazing *color_map* (correct) and several hundred panning *spot_light* (wrong!). Rendering time increases dramatically the more lights you use, so keeping it down to some reasonably small number, say one, would be a better idea.

Technique

Rather than lots of lights, we'll use a single shaped light source known as a *textured_light* that allows us to functionally describe how light surrounds its source, and then tumble the source to splash the interior of a room with shifting light patterns. We'll place this source inside an object that's defined to be the same shape as the distribution of color from the source. It's a cubical, tooth-like, toaster shaped object used in an article by Don Mitchell and Pat Hanrahan on the illumination of curved reflectors for the 1992 SIGGRAPH Proceedings. We'll use a moving *color_map* to paint the walls, making them appear to crawl right out of the floor, looking like badly overexposed tie-dyed T-shirts. This animation uses way too much color. Tables, each with their own spotlight, and an exit door (to allow any remnants of good taste to leave) complete the image.

Steps

We use a box object for our room that's 10 units by 10 units with a ceiling 5 units up. This must either be a metric bar or more a club house than a night club. We generate a fairly intense *color_map* called *ripple_rainbow_texture* that will be mapped onto the entire box. A checkered floor is added. Circular tables are made with a disc, a large cylinder in the form of a band for the table edges, and a smaller diameter pillar to support them both. Six copies are

Technique

This animation was inspired by the terrific tunnel fly-throughs of Chris Smotherman. A view of the tunnel we're building is shown in Figure 3-6.

The tunnel is composed of two perpendicular sets of three parallel cylindrical blobs, basically a square with opposite sides connected like cross hairs (see Figure 3-7). Control points (43 open circles) are scattered around the tunnel, and the QuickBasic program generates a smoothed path near these points (dotted line) as a series of 43 individual segments. The circles appearing on this dotted line are actually the endpoints of each individual segment that smoothly join together to form the path.

The program writes two files during the calculations. The file CUBIC.INC is the collection of the cubic coefficients for each segment, and SPLINE.3D is a file that can be viewed with Oscar Garcia's real time mouse controlled wire

Figure 3-7 Spline path through a tunnel composed of cylindrical blobs

frame 3-D viewer, 3DV. The coefficient files allow us to create the individual camera positions (10 per segment) inside Polyray, rather than resorting to batched *include* files.

Steps

The first step is to place this model on a grid and decide where we want the path to go. The only way to generate the individual control points is to choose them manually. We'll modify certain portions of the path later programmatically, but for starters, you have to decide where the camera should go.

The following code (PATH.BAS) re-creates Figure 3-6 (in color this time) and writes CUBIC.INC (which contains the cubic coefficients for regenerating the spline sections within Polyray), and SPLINE.3D (the 3DV-viewable spline path).

```
' PATH.BAS - Spline Path Creation Program

i = 100
DIM x(i), y(i), z(i)
DIM red(16), green(16), blue(16)

'rainbow palette

DATA  0,  0,  0
DATA 32,  0,  0
DATA 42,  0,  0
DATA 58, 16,  0
DATA 63, 32,  0
DATA 58, 56,  0
DATA 16, 42,  0
DATA  0, 30, 36
DATA  0, 20, 40
DATA  0, 10, 48
DATA  0,  0, 63
DATA 20,  0, 53
DATA 23,  0, 29
DATA 19,  7, 17
DATA 50, 40, 45
DATA 63, 63, 63

SCREEN 12
WINDOW (-10, -7.5)-(10, 7.5)

FOR y = 1 TO 4
      FOR x = 1 TO 4
             colornum = x + ((y - 1) * 4) - 1
             READ red(colornum), green(colornum), blue(colornum)
             KOLOR = 65536 * blue(colornum) + 256 * green(colornum) +
red(colornum)
```

continued on next page

continued from previous page

```
'OPEN "accel" FOR OUTPUT AS #1
FOR x = -6 TO 6 STEP 1
    CIRCLE (x, 0), .25, 4
NEXT x
FOR a = .20 TO .30 STEP .001
LOCATE 1, 1: PRINT a
x = -7
v = 1
DO WHILE x < 6.5
    CIRCLE (x, 1), .15, 2
  '  PRINT #1, x
    x = x + v
    LOCATE 2, 1: PRINT v

  ' accelerate halfway, then decelerate
    IF x < 0 THEN
        v = v + a
    ELSE
        v = v - a
    END IF

LOOP
LOCATE 22, 10: PRINT "PRESS A DEY TO STEP TO THE NEXT VALUE, CTRL-BREAK TO END"
DO WHILE INKEY$ = "": LOOP
LINE (-6.5, .5)-(6.5, 1.5), 0, BF
NEXT a
'CLOSE #1
```

The desired goal was to generate an acceleration/deceleration curve that smoothly meshed with the existing linear spline curve at the endpoints. A loop was set up where the acceleration (*a*) varied over a small range, and the resulting points were displayed above the existing linear ones. When the endpoints lined up, the values for the positions of the acceleration/deceleration points could be used to write new spline control points by changing (*a*) in the code and enabling the PRINT #1 code.

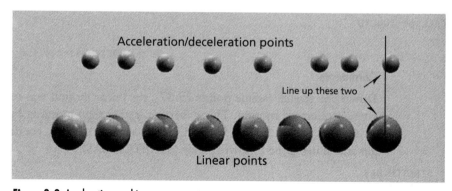

Figure 3-8 Acceleration meshing program output

3.5 How do I...

Simulate motion down an endless tunnel with a simple model and a few frames?

You'll find the code for this in: PLY\CHAPTER3\FAKE

Problem

Let's produce an animation where we run down a very long hallway very fast. Long tunnels that stretch off into vanishing points containing details like doorways, adjoining tunnels, and ceiling lights must contain enormous numbers of graphics primitives. The foreground details have to be repeated until the end of the tunnel is just a guess, a few pixels across. Large numbers of objects can take an awfully long time to render.

A solution that speeds up rendering time and simplifies the modeling uses strategic placement of mirrors both in front of and behind the camera, and allows infinite reflections to create the illusion of a tunnel that stretches on forever (Figure 3-9).

Technique

Barber shops used to have parallel mirrors on their walls to allow you to see the back of your head while you had your hair cut. The reflections stretched on forever, but your face usually got in the way, and impurities and imperfections in the glass limited the range. Fortunately, ray tracers have

Figure 3-9 Fake endless tunnel

perfect mirrors and you don't have to worry about the camera getting in the way because it's invisible. Objects placed between two parallel mirrors will repeat forever, giving the illusion of a world filled with them, extending off into infinity. All we'll need is a short piece of hallway that has exactly the same geometry from one end to the center as it does from the center to the far end. We place mirrors at both ends, and start with the camera just in front of one mirror. We move the camera down the corridor until we're almost touching the other mirror at the far end. With the correct choice of camera steps, the animation will repeat perfectly, and continuous motion down a corridor will be achieved.

Steps

We're after a tunnel that extends forever in front of the camera, or at least far enough so you can't see the end. For contrast, let's start off doing it the hard way, with a physical model that repeats the same tunnel geometry 20 times. In the following listing (REAL.PI), we construct walls from thin boxes (like drywall), map repeating patterns onto them, then cruise off down the hall the distance of one repeating unit in ten frames:

```
// REAL.PI - Image-mapped Endless Tunnel with a Real Tunnel
//    we'll use three targa files as image maps (any will do):
//    the floor - floor.tga
//    the walls - walls.tga
//    the ceiling - ceiling.tga
//    they can be the ones supplied or anything you wish.

start_frame 0
end_frame 9
total_frames 10

outfile "real"

include "\ply\colors.inc"


// move the camera 5 units forward each frame
viewpoint {
   from <0,6,-10+frame*5>
   at <0,0,200+frame*5>
   up <0,1,0>
   angle 30
   resolution 320,200
   aspect 1.6
   }

background midnightblue
```

```
define dim 0.6


define disc_image1 image("floor.tga")
define the_floor
   texture {
      special surface {
         color planar_imagemap(disc_image1, P, 1)
         ambient 0.2
         diffuse 0.8
      }
      translate <-0.5, 0, -0.5>
      scale <1,1,1> -rotate <0,0,90>
   }

define disc_image2 image("walls.tga")
define the_walls
   texture {
      special surface {
         color planar_imagemap(disc_image2, P, 1)
         ambient 0.2
         diffuse 0.8
      }
      translate <-0.5, 0, -0.5>
      rotate <0.0.90>
      scale <1,1,1>
   }

define disc_image3 image("ceiling.tga")
define the_ceiling
   texture {
      special surface {
         color planar_imagemap(disc_image2, P, 1)
         ambient 0.2
         diffuse 0.8
      }
      translate <-0.5, 0, -0.5>
      scale <6,6,6>
   }

// floor
object{
   polygon 4, <-26,0.-26>, <-26,26>, <26,0,26> <26,0,-26>
   the_floor
   }

// wall's
define wall_seg
object {
   object { box < -5,-1, -21>, <-4, 8, 21> stucco }
 + object { box <  4,-1, -21>, < 5, 8, 21> stucco }
 + object { box <-21,-1, -20>, <-4, 8, 21> stucco }
```

continued on next page

continued from previous page

```
            ambient 0.2
            diffuse 0.8
        }
        translate <-0.5, 0, -0.5>
        scale <6,6,6>
    }

define reflector
texture {
    surface {
        ambient white, 0
        diffuse white, 0
        specular 0
        reflection white, 1
        }
    }

// wall's
define wall
    object {
        object { box < -5,-1, -4>, <-4.1, 9, -26> the_walls }
      + object { box <  4.1,-1, -4>, <5, 9,-26> the_walls }
    }

define hall
    object {
        wall {rotate <0,  0,0>}
      + wall {rotate <0, 90,0>}
      + wall {rotate <0,180,0>}
      + wall {rotate <0,270,0>}    .
}

if(overhead_view==no)
// ceiling
object {
    polygon 4, <-26,8,-26>,<-26,8,26>,<26,8,26>,<26,8,-26>
    the_ceiling
    }
}

// floor
object {
    polygon 4, <-26,0,-26>,<-26,0,26>,<26,0,26>,<26,0,-26>
    the_floor
    }

define bright_white
texture {
    surface {
        ambient 0.3
        diffuse 0.7
        color <2,2,2>
```

```
        }
}

define fixture
object {
    box <-3,7.8,-3>, <3, 8, 3>
    bright_white
    }

hall

fixture
fixture {translate < 25,0, 0>}
fixture {translate <-25,0, 0>}
fixture {translate <  0,0, 25>}
fixture {translate <  0,0,-25>}

define dim 0.5

light white*dim,<0,7,0>

light white*dim,<24,7,0>
light white*dim,<-24,7,0>
light white*dim,<0,7,24>
light white*dim,<0,7,-24>

define mirror1
    object {
        polygon 4, <-5,-1,0>,<5,-1,0>,<5,9,0>,<-5,9,0>
        translate <0,0,-25>
        reflector
}

mirror1 {rotate <0,  0,0>}
mirror1 {rotate <0, 90,0>}
mirror1 {rotate <0,180,0>}
mirror1 {rotate <0,270,0>}
```

How It Works

Our sections are 50 units long, running from -25 to 25. Start with the camera at -22.5, then step it 5 units forward each frame. The last frame is at 22.5, again 2.5 units away from the mirror. The next step would place us the equivalent of -22.5 in the next segment, which means the animation will loop perfectly.

This animation is the first one in which a lot of texture maps are used, so a few words about them are in order. Other than obvious stuff like scaling, the only parameter to keep in mind is the angle they make with the item they'll be mapped onto. By default, images map onto the *x-z* plane. If you want to map them onto walls, be sure to rotate them about x or z (whichever is appropriate for your model), otherwise you'll map a long thin section of your image across the surface, which may not be what you're after. You can use any image at all for the texture maps, as well as the ones that are included.

Many of the items in this model are defined first, and then copied and used several times. This is not only easy to code, but it also ensures that the model will repeat exactly as it should. The model is simply four corridors rotated about a central space. The rotation is an important part of the modeling. If the walls and floor have conspicuous texture maps, they will not tile properly unless the pattern meets at the mirror points, and a rotation is the simplest way of achieving this. It also helps to have a neutral texture. It makes hiding the mirror points easier.

Comments

You can set the number of times Polyray reflects scenes off mirrors with the *max_level* parameter in the POLYRAY.INI file. It's usually 10 or 20, and it definitely matters in this sort of image. If you want to approach the end of the tunnel and break out into some other animation, try reducing this parameter by one for each series of frames. You'll be able to see the end of the tunnel approaching, and break on through to the other side.

3.6 How do I...
Create a bubbling mud-bog surface?

You'll find the code for this in: PLY\CHAPTER3\BOG

Problem

A few years back, it seemed like almost every high-end math visualization and statistics package used the sombrero function as eye-catchers in their ads to show how good they were at making neat 3-D meshes (Figure 3-11). It's a nice shape, but it basically only does one thing. How would you make an extended surface pocketed with these functions erupt at staggered intervals?

Technique

The answer is, you play with the math and you get lucky. Trigonometry is neat stuff. It deals with the ratios of the length of the sides of triangles, but

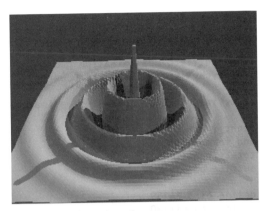

Figure 3-11 The sombrero function

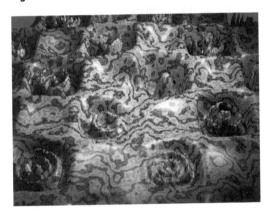

Figure 3-12 Bog surface

the factors involved do wonderful things. Take, for instance, the following equation:

$$sin(2 * (r+frame)^{(cos(x) * sin(z))}) * sin(a * 4 * rad))$$

where

$$r = (x^2+z^2)^{0.5}$$
$$a = acos(x/r)$$

Know what it does? Neither do I. Haven't the foggiest. It came from an afternoon session of playing with equations and seeing the effects of putting sines, cosines, and powers at random positions in an equation. A high boredom threshold comes in handy at times. But seriously, what it actually does is creates a bubbly surface that's really bad on the eyes (see Figure 3-12).

continued from previous page

```
spot_light <1,0,1>, < 0,0,-100>,<0,0,0>,3,5,20

define pop1 3*frame/30
define pop2 3*sin(3*frame*rad)

if (frame < 30) {
   object { sphere <0,0,0>,pop1 matte_white }
}
if (frame < 60) {
   object { sphere <0,0,0>,pop2 matte_white }
}

define c0000 < -1.00000, -2.88675,-11.43095>
if ( |c0000| < size) {
   object { sphere c0000, 1  matte_white }
}
define c0001 <  1.00000, -2.88675,-11.43095>
if ( |c0001| < size) {
   object { sphere c0001, 1  matte_white }
}
define c0002 < -2.00000, -1.15470,-11.43095>
if ( |c0002| < size) {
   object { sphere c0002, 1  matte_white }
}
define c0003 <  0.00000, -1.15470,-11.43095>
if ( |c0003| < size) {
   object { sphere c0003, 1  matte_white }
}
define c0004 <  2.00000, -1.15470,-11.43095>
if ( |c0004| < size) {
   object { sphere c0004, 1  matte_white }
}
define c0005 < -3.00000,  0.57735,-11.43095>
if ( |c0005| < size) {
   object { sphere c0005, 1  matte_white }
}
define c0006 < -1.00000,  0.57735,-11.43095>
if ( |c0006| < size) {
   object { sphere c0006, 1  matte_white }
}
define c0007 <  1.00000,  0.57735,-11.43095>
if ( |c0007| < size) {
   object { sphere c0007, 1  matte_white }
}
define c0008 <  3.00000,  0.57735,-11.43095>
if ( |c0008| < size) {
   object { sphere c0008, 1  matte_white }
}
...
```

An example of what we're generating is shown in Figure 3-15.

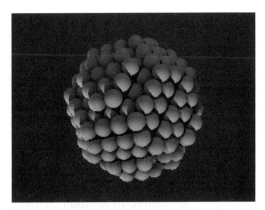

Figure 3-15 A growing mass of spheres

How It Works

The growth is handled using Polyray's vector length function |*vexper*|. The variable *size* grows outward each frame

```
define size 12*frame/total_frames
```

and sets the size of the decision sphere. If the length of the vector defining the position of the sphere is less than *size,* the object sphere will pop into view in our image.

The code created by this QuickBasic program is rather lengthy, as there are 1,250 spheres in the array. The listing was abbreviated.

Two Decision Spheres

This animation renders quickly, but it's still not quite as smooth as we'd like. A smoother way of growing the sphere without "spackle" requires using two decision spheres, one twice the size of the other. The second sphere brings in elements before they would normally appear in the scene, but scaled down so that they don't overtake the primary sphere growth. They fill in the cracks. As the decision sphere expands, we enlarge and position these spheres back to their original size. They then take the positions they would have if we had used a single decision sphere. This is all handled by a second *if* clause shown in this excerpt:

```
define c0000  < -1.00000, -2.88675,-11.43095>
if ( |c0000| < size) {
    object { sphere c0000, 1  matte_white }
}
// 2 times the previous decision sphere
if ( |c0000| < size*2) {
    object { sphere c0000*size/|c0000|, 1  matte_white }
}
```

CHAPTER THREE

```
// MOOSE.PI
// Moose Shaped Blob Reflection Deal

include "\ply\colors.inc"

start_frame 0
end_frame 89
total_frames 90
define index 360/total_frames

outfile "moose"

viewpoint {
   from <0.8,0.8,0.0>
   at <0.0,0.0,0.0>
   up <0,1,0>
   angle 90
   resolution 320,200
   aspect 1.433
   }

background SkyBlue
light <0.7,0.7,0.7>,<10,12,1>
define ang frame*index

define unit_sphere object { sphere <0, 0, 0>, 1.0 }

define eye
   object {
      object {
         sphere <0.0,0.0,0.0>,0.10
         texture {
            surface {
               ambient red, 0.2
               diffuse red, 0.5
               specular white, 0.7
            }
         }
      }
   +  object {
         sphere <0.0,0.0,0.0>,0.05
         texture {
            surface {
               ambient Yellow, 0.5
               diffuse Coral, 0.8
               specular white, 0.9
            }
         }
      translate <0.05,0.05,0.0 >
      }
   }

define weird_shape
```

176

```
object {
   blob 6.6:
      7, 3.0,<  0,  0,  0 >,
      3, 1.0,<  1,  1,  1 >,
      3, 1.0,< -1,  1,  1 >,
      3, 1.0,<  1, -1,  1 >,
      3, 1.0,< -1, -1,  1 >,
      3, 1.0,<  1,  1, -1 >,
      3, 1.0,< -1,  1, -1 >,
      3, 1.0,<  1, -1, -1 >,
      3, 1.0,< -1, -1, -1 >,
      3, 1.0,<  0,  1,  1 >,
      3, 1.0,<  0,  1, -1 >,
      3, 1.0,<  0, -1,  1 >,
      3, 1.0,<  0, -1, -1 >,
      3, 1.0,<  1,  0,  1 >,
      3, 1.0,<  1,  0, -1 >,
      3, 1.0,< -1,  0,  1 >,
      3, 1.0,< -1,  0, -1 >,
      3, 1.0,<  1,  1,  0 >,
      3, 1.0,<  1, -1,  0 >,
      3, 1.0,< -1,  1,  0 >,
      3, 1.0,< -1, -1,  0 >
   root_solver Sturm
   u_steps 20
   v_steps 20
   reflective_coral
   }

object {
   weird_shape & unit_sphere
   rotate <45.0,ang,0.0>
   }


eye {
   rotate <70,70,30>
   translate <0.25,0.25,0.25>
   rotate <0.0,ang,0.0>
   }

eye {
   rotate <10,-10,0>
   translate <0.25,0.25,-0.25>
   rotate <0.0,ang,0.0>
   }
```

CHAPTER

4

continued from previous page

```
include "\PLY\COLORS.INC"

define mirror2
texture {
   surface {
      ambient gold, 0.1
      diffuse white, 0.2
      specular 0
      reflection white, 1
      }
   }

// set up background color & lights
background SkyBlue

// a coral colored light
light <1,0.5,0>,<0,10,0>

define pi 3.14159
define rad pi/180

// make the wave front collapse and then expand

if (frame <40)
   define wave_radius cos((frame)*4.8*rad) + 1
else
   define wave_radius (frame-40)/20

define phase_in -(0.75+0.65*(frame-20)/30)

//start with a flat surface, indent and rebound, then decay

if (frame <20)
   define height 0
else if (frame <50)
   define height phase_in*sin(9 * (frame - 20) * rad)
else
   define height 5/exp(frame/40)

// heightfield is a radially symmetrical expanding gaussian

define width  0.3
define r (x^2+z^2)^0.5

define HFn height / EXP(((r - wave_radius) / width) ^ 2)
define detail 100
// define the wave surface
object {
    smooth_height_fn detail, detail, -10, 10, -10, 10, HFn
    mirror2
    }
```

```
// drop an expanding ball on it

define ball (23-frame)/7.5
define grow 0.25+0.25*frame/20

object {
   sphere <0,ball,0>,grow
   shiny_coral
   }

// give the surface something hidden to reflect

object {
  disc <0, 20, 0>, <0, 1, 0>, 20
    texture {
       checker matte_white, matte_black
       translate <0, -0.1, 0>
       scale <2, 1, 2>
       }
   }
```

The QuickBasic code and the Polyray code are identical in the way they achieve the various stages of this animation. Conditional processing sets the times when key actions occur, like the change in the diameter of the splash ring and its rise and fall.

The surface is defined using the *height* and *wave_radius* variables generated by all this conditional code, defined as the variable *HFn,* which is included at the end of a *smooth_height_fn* definition. The *detail* variable sets the level of smoothness, or the number of subdivisions the heightfield uses to approximate the surface. Polyray calculates heights for a square running from -10 to 10 in both *x* and *z:*

```
define width  0.3
define r (x^2+z^2)^0.5

define HFn height / EXP(((r - wave_radius) / width) ^ 2)
define detail 100
// define the wave surface
object {
    smooth_height_fn detail, detail, -10, 10, -10, 10, HFn
    mirror2
    }
```

All this motion is coordinated with dropping a ball on the surface. It touches the surface at frame 20, but its center doesn't make it through until frame 23:

```
define ball (23-frame)/7.5
define grow 0.25+0.25*frame/20
```

The ball is visible as a reflection on the surface before it comes into actual view, and to exaggerate the fall, we expand it as it drops with the *grow* variable that sets its radius. This effect was originally added to reduce its size and keep it hidden at frame 0, since without this scaling, it would suddenly pop into view at the loop point. Later on, the camera was moved and this scaling was no longer required. However the expanding effect was interesting, and so it was kept.

Comments

There are a few interesting twists here. The surface is a mirror that when undisturbed fails to reflect a checkerboard that's been placed up above the camera and out of view. It's only seen in the surface ripples. The lighting creates a coral checkerboard, but has no impact on the color of the mirror.

If the fluid overshoots the indentation once, it should be able to do it several times, producing a damped oscillation. We might attempt to increase the complexity of the heightfield by using our Gaussian function to shape a packet of sine waves. It was simpler to assume that the fluid was very viscous and that a single pulse was all we would get, but don't let that stop you from trying this variation.

4.2 How do I...
Make a diamond swim like a jellyfish?

You'll find the code for this in: PLY\CHAPTER4\JELLYDIM

Problem

Solid objects defined as triangle grids make ideal candidates for 3-D morphs. Coordinated deformations require establishing a framework that collects the points defining the triangles together in groups. These groups are then translated relative to one another using some procedure. The least flexible object in nature is a diamond. It would be interesting to see it swim like a jellyfish.

Technique

If you've ever watched a jellyfish swim, you may have noticed it's not exactly a continuous sine wave motion like a spring. It's more of a heave and a

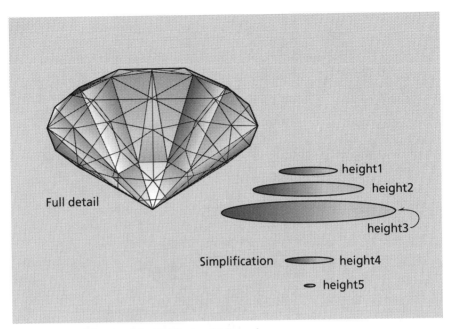

Figure 4-3 The full view and the simplification of a diamond

pause, a heave and a pause. You may have also noticed that different parts of the jellyfish move at different times, so that the relative motions of the parts are *phased*.

We approach this animation in two stages. First, we'll create a real-time simulation of a rough model of our diamond. Then we'll write a diamond generator inside Polyray, exploiting a faceted diamond's eight-way symmetry, and layer the motion on top of this geometry.

Steps

The basic simulation code needs to reduce the complexity of the diamond to a simpler form for a faster running wire frame simulation. A fully detailed diamond wire frame and the simplification we'll use are shown in Figure 4-3.

The simplification breaks the diamond up into five different levels, represented by circles connecting vertices of different levels. A better view of the diamond showing these five different heights is shown in Figure 4-4.

The following code animates the simplified version of the model and allows us to adjust the phase and amplitude of the various components until we're happy with the results:

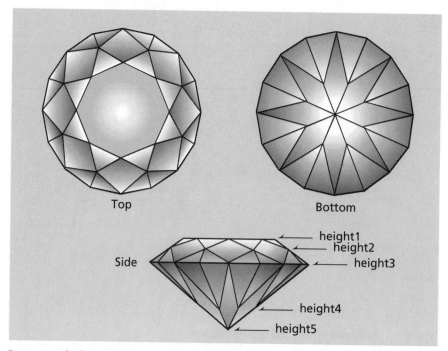

Figure 4-4 The diamond. Coplanar triangles in the full detail view have been collapsed into trapezoids

```
' JellyDim.BAS
' Jellyfish Diamond Motion File
TYPE vector
  x AS SINGLE
  y AS SINGLE
  z AS SINGLE
END TYPE

pi = 3.1415926536#
radians = 180 / pi

DIM vertex(42) AS vector, triangle(3) AS vector
DIM red(16), green(16), blue(16)

' set the screen up with pretty rainbow colors

SCREEN 12

zoom = .015
xoff = 320
yoff = 240

WINDOW ((0 - xoff) * zoom, (0 - yoff) * zoom)-((639 - xoff) * zoom, (479 - ⇐
yoff) * zoom)

FOR y = 1 TO 4
```

```
        FOR x = 1 TO 4
                colornum = x + ((y - 1) * 4) - 1
                READ red(colornum), green(colornum), blue(colornum)
                KOLOR = 65536 * blue(colornum) + 256 * green(colornum) + ⇐
red(colornum)
                PALETTE colornum, KOLOR
                COLOR colornum
        NEXT x
NEXT y


'rainbow palette

DATA  0,  0,  0
DATA 32,  0,  0
DATA 42,  0,  0
DATA 58, 16,  0
DATA 63, 32,  0
DATA 58, 56,  0
DATA 16, 42,  0
DATA  0, 30, 36
DATA  0, 20, 40
DATA  0, 10, 48
DATA  0,  0, 63
DATA 20,  0, 53
DATA 23,  0, 29
DATA 19,  7, 17
DATA 50, 40, 45
DATA 63, 63, 63

pi = 3.1415926535#
rad = pi / 180

radius1 = 1
radius2 = 1.4
radius3 = 1.8
radius4 = .7
radius5 = .01

ht1 = 1
ht2 = .8
ht3 = .5
ht4 = -.5
ht5 = -1

masteramp = 1.3

ampl1 = .03 * masteramp
ampl2 = .02 * masteramp
ampl3 = .01 * masteramp
ampl4 = .04 * masteramp
ampl5 = .05 * masteramp

phase = 80    ' hump phase
```

continued on next page

continued from previous page
```
define vertex33z height4


define f 2
define a 360 * f / 8
define bend2 45

define vertex02x newradius1 * cos(rad * a)
define vertex02y newradius1 * SIN(rad * a)
define vertex02z height1

define vertex10x newradius2 * cos(rad * (a + 22.5))
define vertex10y newradius2 * SIN(rad * (a + 22.5))
define vertex10z height2

define vertex18x newradius3 * cos(rad * (a + 45))
define vertex18y newradius3 * SIN(rad * (a + 45))
define vertex18z height3

define vertex26x newradius3 * cos(rad * (a + 67.5))
define vertex26y newradius3 * SIN(rad * (a + 67.5))
define vertex26z height3

define vertex34x newradius4 * cos(rad * (a + 67.5))
define vertex34y newradius4 * SIN(rad * (a + 67.5))
define vertex34z height4
...
```

DIAM1.PI continues in this fashion until it becomes necessary to define the separate faces of the image. This is handled as shown in this exerpt from DIAM1.PI.

```
// the triangular faces listed clockwise by vertex


define diam
  object {

// Crown

    object { polygon 3,<vertex01x,vertex01y,vertex01z>,<vertex42x,vertex42y,⇐
vertex42z>,<vertex02x,vertex02y,vertex02z>}
  + object { polygon 3,<vertex02x,vertex02y,vertex02z>,<vertex42x,vertex42y,⇐
vertex42z>,<vertex03x,vertex03y,vertex03z>}
  + object { polygon 3,<vertex03x,vertex03y,vertex03z>,<vertex42x,vertex42y,⇐
vertex42z>,<vertex04x,vertex04y,vertex04z>}
  + object { polygon 3,<vertex04x,vertex04y,vertex04z>,<vertex42x,vertex42y,⇐
vertex42z>,<vertex05x,vertex05y,vertex05z>}
  + object { polygon 3,<vertex05x,vertex05y,vertex05z>,<vertex42x,vertex42y,⇐
vertex42z>,<vertex06x,vertex06y,vertex06z>}
```

```
 + object { polygon 3,<vertex06x,vertex06y,vertex06z>,<vertex42x,vertex42y,⇐
vertex42z>,<vertex07x,vertex07y,vertex07z>}
 + object { polygon 3,<vertex07x,vertex07y,vertex07z>,<vertex42x,vertex42y,⇐
vertex42z>,<vertex08x,vertex08y,vertex08z>}
 + object { polygon 3,<vertex08x,vertex08y,vertex08z>,<vertex42x,vertex42y,⇐
vertex42z>,<vertex01x,vertex01y,vertex01z>}
 + object { polygon 3,<vertex01x,vertex01y,vertex01z>,<vertex02x,vertex02y,⇐
vertex02z>,<vertex09x,vertex09y,vertex09z>}
 + object { polygon 3,<vertex02x,vertex02y,vertex02z>,<vertex03x,vertex03y,⇐
vertex03z>,<vertex10x,vertex10y,vertex10z>}
 + object { polygon 3,<vertex03x,vertex03y,vertex03z>,<vertex04x,vertex04y,⇐
vertex04z>,<vertex11x,vertex11y,vertex11z>}
 + object { polygon 3,<vertex04x,vertex04y,vertex04z>,<vertex05x,vertex05y,⇐
vertex05z>,<vertex12x,vertex12y,vertex12z>}
 + object { polygon 3,<vertex05x,vertex05y,vertex05z>,<vertex06x,vertex06y,⇐
vertex06z>,<vertex13x,vertex13y,vertex13z>}
 + object { polygon 3,<vertex06x,vertex06y,vertex06z>,<vertex07x,vertex07y,⇐
vertex07z>,<vertex14x,vertex14y,vertex14z>}
 + object { polygon 3,<vertex07x,vertex07y,vertex07z>,<vertex08x,vertex08y,⇐
vertex08z>,<vertex15x,vertex15y,vertex15z>}
 + object { polygon 3,<vertex08x,vertex08y,vertex08z>,<vertex01x,vertex01y,⇐
vertex01z>,<vertex16x,vertex16y,vertex16z>}
...

diam {rotate <0,0,ang/8>
      translate <0,0,-1.5+height1>}
```

The motion has already been covered in the QuickBasic simulation code. It translates without a hitch. Keeping track of all the vertices may be tedious, but number the vertices in Figure 4-4, starting with the top octagon 1 through 8, then 9 through 16 for the next ring, and so on up to 40, then number the bottom point 41 and the center of the top octagon 42, and you have it. This allows you to keep track of the 42 control vertices. Then it becomes just a matter of calling up each triangle in clockwise order from the outside, although providing you're consistent, (clockwise or counterclockwise, pick one), it doesn't matter. A sample image is shown if Figure 4-7.

Comments

Changing the ratio of the magnitude of *bump* to *wave* produces a range of motions, from a rubber spring-like up-and-down oscillation to a periodic pulse. The exponent in the *bump* term limits the acceptable values for *bump* to a maximum of about 1.3, although watching it go non-linear can also be amusing.

continued from previous page

```
include "\PLY\COLORS.INC"

// set up background color & lights
background midnightblue

define dim 1

light <1,0,0>*dim,< 10,  0,  0>
light <1,1,1>*dim,<  0, 10,  0>
light <0,0,1>*dim,<  0,  0, 10>

light <1,1,0>*dim,<-10,  0,  0>
light <0,1,1>*dim,<  0,-10,  0>
light <1,0,1>*dim,<  0,  0,-10>


viewpoint {
   from <3, 6, 4>
   at <0,0,0>
   up   <0, 1,  0>
   angle 30
   resolution 320,200
   aspect 1.43
   }

// the phased breathing terms

define ph1 1+0.5*cos(index*rad)    // goes from 0.5 to 1.5
define ph2 0.5*(1+0.5*sin(index*rad))  // goes from 0.25 to 0.75


// valleys ("F"ace Centers)
define f01 <0,1,1>*ph1
define f02 <1,0,1>*ph1
define f03 <0,-1,1>*ph1
define f04 <-1,0,1>*ph1

// peaks ("T"ips)
define t01 <1,1,1>*ph2
define t02 <1,-1,1>*ph2
define t03 <-1,-1,1>*ph2
define t04 <-1,1,1>*ph2

// "C"entral point
define c01 <0,0,1>

define face
   object {
      object { polygon 3, f01,t01,c01 matte_white}
    + object { polygon 3, t01,f02,c01 matte_white}
    + object { polygon 3, f02,t02,c01 matte_white}
    + object { polygon 3, t02,f03,c01 matte_white}
    + object { polygon 3, f03,t03,c01 matte_white}
```

```
   + object { polygon 3, t03,f04,c01 matte_white}
   + object { polygon 3, f04,t04,c01 matte_white}
   + object { polygon 3, t04,f01,c01 matte_white}
   }

define star
   object {
      face
   + face { rotate <0, 90,0> }
   + face { rotate <0,180,0> }
   + face { rotate <0,270,0> }
   + face { rotate <90, 0,0> }
   + face { rotate <270,0,0> }
   }

star {rotate <index,45*sin(2*index*rad),90*cos(index*rad)>}
```

How It Works

There were two classes of points, peaks, or tips (*t*) and valleys or face centers (*f* and *c*). The motions of the centers and tips are phased 90° apart, and *ph1* has twice the magnitude of *ph2*, making it easy to tell the difference between the two as each set takes center stage. The figure expands to a star, contracts to a ball, extrudes into connected plates, and then returns to the star shape (see Figure 4-10).

Figure 4-10 Moravian star in four configurations

Comments

This entire figure is defined by eight vertices and one central point. Simple rotations of these points can result in all sorts of interesting shape changes. To rotate the tips:

```
// peaks ("T"ips)
define t01 rotate(<1,1,1>*ph2, <0,0,45*sin(3*index*rad)>)
define t02 rotate(<1,-1,1>*ph2,<0,0,45*sin(3*index*rad)>)
define t03 rotate(<-1,-1,1>*ph2,<0,0,45*sin(3*index*rad)>)
define t04 rotate(<-1,1,1>*ph2,<0,0,45*sin(3*index*rad)>)
```

We can also change the phase (relative timing) of the in-and-out motions for members of each symmetrical set, but due to pre-existing symmetry constraints, the figure will no longer be solid. Cracks will appear between the segments. This isn't necessarily a bad thing, though.

While this is a simple example of triangle mesh morphing, the same principle can be applied to far more complex objects. You can purchase triangle and polygon mesh models for things like tennis shoes and busts of Beethoven. The vertices can be moved using functions based on their distance from strategically placed control points, and morphed into all sorts of interesting shapes.

4.4 How do I...
Morph functionally defined objects?

You'll find the code for this in: PLY\CHAPTER4\CARB

Problem

In the previous animation (STAR.PI), we dealt with the periodic displacements of the discrete vertices controlling the shape of a solid object defined as a triangle mesh. It's also possible to take a functionally defined object and modify the function to do the same type of thing. Let's take the cubical object from the Disco Inferno animation (Section 3.3) and blow out its sides sequentially as we rotate it.

Technique

Functionally defined objects get their shapes from solving the equations that define their surfaces. Such is the case with the tooth-like object we used in Section 3.3, based on an object from an article by Don Mitchell and Pat Hanrahan in the 1992 SIGGRAPH Proceedings on the illumination of curved reflectors. The object is defined where points on its surface solve the relationship:

$$x^4 + y^4 + z^4 - x^2 - y^{\wedge}2 - z^2 = 0$$

For example, the points <1,1,1>, <-1,-1,-1> and in fact the other six corners of a unit cube all satisfy this equation. The in-between points are what's hard to see what's going on intuitively. Polyray gets its name from its ability to ray trace objects defined by polynomials, so this is right up its alley.

In order to change the shape of this object, we need to add additional factors indexed by the frame count that move this surface around. We do so by multiplying *x*, *y*, and *z* by three new variables *a*, *b*, and *c*. In code this is handled:

```
define m 360/total_frames
define off sin(frame*m*8*rad)/2

define a (sin(frame*m*rad)+off)/2
define b (sin((frame*m+120)*rad)+off)/2
define c (sin((frame*m+240)*rad)+off)/2
...
polynomial a*x^4 + b*y^4 + c*z^4 - a*x^2 - b*y^2 - c*z^2
```

These new variables shift the solution for the surface so that it opens up revealing interesting interior details that resemble a four barrel carburetor— so we've named the device CARB (see Figure 4-11).

Polyray Code

CARB is a multi-ported, topologically varied object. (It has a variable number of holes in it.) Simulating functionally defined surfaces inside QuickBasic is extremely difficult. It requires an accelerated solution to find

Figure 4-11 Our carburetor

example of this kind of lettering, but understandably, companies like IBM are very proud of their logos. The thought of having thousands of twisting, wiggling, raving polka dot IBM logos bouncing around every bulletin board from Armonk to Anchorage caused them some concern. So instead, we'll opt for things that make you go "HMM." These are the initials of my research director at Virginia Tech, Dr. Harold M. McNair. Those initials always made it ambiguous whether a document was something he was wondering about, or something he had written.

Technique

The classic Steam Boat Willie cartoon of the 30s had almost every object in the scene bouncing up and down in time with the music. Apparently, Willie himself must have been two-cycle, since he bounced twice as fast as he walked. We're going to animate the letters HMM to give it this type of bounce, swaying back and forth, moving past the camera in a motion known as "happy-train." We'll refrain from making it whistle, though.

First generate the letters, using QuickBasic to do the nasty low-level stuff. The procedure involves sketching out letters on graph paper and deriving the controlling vertices for the various blocks. Concentrate on finding critical points: things like corners, centers of circles (none here, but keep it in mind for your logos), things that line up, distances... and manually extract as much information as possible. Any regularities in the letters are exploited to simplify the creation of the model. In this particular case, each letter contained regularly spaced horizontal stripes, many of which line up vertically. This extracted data is placed into DATA statements and called in loops to convert it into boxes and polygons, the elements of our logo. The following code (HM.BAS) displays both the letters as they're created and writes a Polyray file defining the blocks.

Boxes suffice for some of the pieces, but for slanted sections of the M that aren't square, polygons must be used six at a time to construct trapezoidal enclosures. The code creates an include file called HM.INC with each piece of each letter named *H1-H8* and *M1-M8*, and displays the letters on the screen (see Figure 4-17). We needn't make two *M's*; we can translate a copy of the first *M* to make a second one.

QuickBasic Code

The following program generates the letters in Figure 4-18. It uses blocks of data statements and regularities inside the letters themselves to make the final model. Again, the code is long and has been abbreviated here. Check the file for the complete listing.

Figure 4-17 The letters HM in sliced bread font

```
' HM.BAS - Creates two block letters H and M

SCREEN 12
WINDOW SCREEN (-20, -50)-(299.5, 189.5)

OPEN "hm.inc" FOR OUTPUT AS #1

'depth

z1 = -50
z2 = 50

'H - left side

DATA 31,65
DATA 31,65
DATA 44,65
DATA 44,115
DATA 44,115
DATA 44,65
DATA 31,65
DATA 31,65

FOR i = 1 TO 8
READ x1, x2
y1 = (i - 1) * 13
y2 = (i - 1) * 13 + 7
LINE (x1, y1)-(x2, y2), 15, B

Name$ = RIGHT$("HL" + LTRIM$(STR$(i)), 3)
Center$ = RIGHT$("HLC" + LTRIM$(STR$(i)), 4)

PRINT #1, "define "; Name$
PRINT #1, "object {"
PRINT #1, USING "  box <###.##, ###.##, ###.##>, <###.##, ###.##, ###.##>"; ⇐
x1, y1, z1, x2, y2, z2
```

continued on next page

the coordinates (0,0). Positive values flood the rest of the screen. This means that letters are upside down. The final code should make them sway so the sections closest to the axes remain steady and sections farther out sway. In other words, these letters will sway like kids on monkey bars (top stable/bottom swaying) rather than an overloaded truck (bottom stable/top swaying), which is what we're after. Rather than recollect the data, we can rectify this situation by flipping the normal "up" vector from <0,1,0> to <0,-1,0> and call the blocks defining each slice of the letters in reverse order (*H8* -> *H1* rather than *H1* -> *H8*), as shown:

```
define H8 object { HL1 + HR1 }
define H7 object { HL2 + HR2 }
define H6 object { HL3 + HR3 }
define H5 object { HL4 }
define H4 object { HL5 }
define H3 object { HL6 + HR6 }
define H2 object { HL7 + HR7 }
define H1 object { HL8 + HR8 }
```

Polyray Data File

The following Polyray data file (HMM.PI) uses the geometry in the *include* file HM.INC, built from the QuickBasic code file, to construct our happy-train HMM logo.

```
// HMM.PI - Happy-Train Letters

start_frame 0
end_frame 162
total_frames 163

outfile "HMM"

viewpoint {
   from <55,25,300>
   at <125,55,0>
   up <0,-1,0>
   angle 30
   resolution 160,120
   aspect 1.333
   }
include "\PLY\COLORS.INC"

define Ochre <0.6,0.3,0.0>
background Ochre
light white, < -50,-100,250>
light white, < 300,-100,250>

include "hm.inc"
```

```
define H8 object { HL1 + HR1 }
define H7 object { HL2 + HR2 }
define H6 object { HL3 + HR3 }
define H5 object { HL4 }
define H4 object { HL5 }
define H3 object { HL6 + HR6 }
define H2 object { HL7 + HR7 }
define H1 object { HL8 + HR8 }


define M8 object { ML1 + MR1 }
define M7 object { ML2 + MR2 }
define M6 object { ML3 + MR3 }
define M5 object { ML4 + MML4 + MMR4 + MR4 }
define M4 object { ML5 + MM5 + MR5 }
define M3 object { ML6 + MM6 + MR6 }
define M2 object { ML7 + MM7 + MR7 }
define M1 object { ML8 + MM8 + MR8 }

define M28 object { ML1 + MR1 translate <131,0,0>}
define M27 object { ML2 + MR2 translate <131,0,0>}
define M26 object { ML3 + MR3 translate <131,0,0>}
define M25 object { ML4 + MML4 + MMR4 + MR4 translate <131,0,0>}
define M24 object { ML5 + MM5 + MR5 translate <131,0,0>}
define M23 object { ML6 + MM6 + MR6 translate <131,0,0>}
define M22 object { ML7 + MM7 + MR7 translate <131,0,0>}
define M21 object { ML8 + MM8 + MR8 translate <131,0,0>}

define major 0.2
define minor 0.05
define spacing 13

define pi 3.14159
define rad pi/180

define Y1 0* spacing * major * sin(frame*24*rad)
define Y2 1* spacing * major * sin(frame*24*rad)
define Y3 2* spacing * major * sin(frame*24*rad)
define Y4 3* spacing * major * sin(frame*24*rad)
define Y5 4* spacing * major * sin(frame*24*rad)
define Y6 5* spacing * major * sin(frame*24*rad)
define Y7 6* spacing * major * sin(frame*24*rad)
define Y8 7* spacing * major * sin(frame*24*rad)


define amp 2.5

define xr1 0 * amp * sin(rad * frame * 6)
define xr2 1 * amp * sin(rad * frame * 6)
define xr3 2 * amp * sin(rad * frame * 6)
define xr4 3 * amp * sin(rad * frame * 6)
define xr5 4 * amp * sin(rad * frame * 6)
define xr6 5 * amp * sin(rad * frame * 6)
define xr7 6 * amp * sin(rad * frame * 6)
```

continued on next page

continued from previous page

```
define xr8 7 * amp * sin(rad * frame * 6)

define train 270-frame*4

H1 {translate <train, Y1, 0> rotate <xr1,0,0> }
H2 {translate <train, Y2, 0> rotate <xr2,0,0> }
H3 {translate <train, Y3, 0> rotate <xr3,0,0> }
H4 {translate <train, Y4, 0> rotate <xr4,0,0> }
H5 {translate <train, Y5, 0> rotate <xr5,0,0> }
H6 {translate <train, Y6, 0> rotate <xr6,0,0> }
H7 {translate <train, Y7, 0> rotate <xr7,0,0> }
H8 {translate <train, Y8, 0> rotate <xr8,0,0> }

M1 {translate <train, Y1, 0> rotate <-xr1,0,0> }
M2 {translate <train, Y2, 0> rotate <-xr2,0,0> }
M3 {translate <train, Y3, 0> rotate <-xr3,0,0> }
M4 {translate <train, Y4, 0> rotate <-xr4,0,0> }
M5 {translate <train, Y5, 0> rotate <-xr5,0,0> }
M6 {translate <train, Y6, 0> rotate <-xr6,0,0> }
M7 {translate <train, Y7, 0> rotate <-xr7,0,0> }
M8 {translate <train, Y8, 0> rotate <-xr8,0,0> }

M21 {translate <train, Y1, 0> rotate <xr1,0,0> }
M22 {translate <train, Y2, 0> rotate <xr2,0,0> }
M23 {translate <train, Y3, 0> rotate <xr3,0,0> }
M24 {translate <train, Y4, 0> rotate <xr4,0,0> }
M25 {translate <train, Y5, 0> rotate <xr5,0,0> }
M26 {translate <train, Y6, 0> rotate <xr6,0,0> }
M27 {translate <train, Y7, 0> rotate <xr7,0,0> }
M28 {translate <train, Y8, 0> rotate <xr8,0,0> }
```

The left, middle, and right portions of each character are first grouped together to form single named coplanar objects (*H1-H8*, *M1-M8*, and *M21-M28*) that will move as units under rotations and translations. A copy of the first M is made and moved 131 units to the right to form the second one. As we mentioned earlier, the top-down order has been reversed to compensate for the way the letters were originally defined.

Two motions are imparted to these slices. First, each slice bounces up and down with simple harmonic motion every 15 frames (15*24=360°) using the variables *Y1-Y8*:

```
define major 0.2
define spacing 13

define Y1 0* spacing * major * sin(frame*24*rad)
define Y2 1* spacing * major * sin(frame*24*rad)
...
```

Next, the letters are made to rock front-to-back every 30 frames (30*6 = 360°) with varying amplitude, from 0° at the base for a stable platform to ±17.5° at the top (2.5*7 = 17.5°):

Figure 4-18 HMM train

```
define amp 2.5

define xr1 0 * amp * sin(rad * frame * 6)
define xr2 1 * amp * sin(rad * frame * 6)
...
define xr8 7 * amp * sin(rad * frame * 6)
```

Finally, the letters run past the camera at a rate of 4 units per frame using the variable *train*. For simplicity, we combine *train* with the up-and-down translation (*Y1-Y8*) in a single step:

```
define train 270-frame*4
...translate <train,Y1,0>...
```

A frame from the middle of the HMM.PI is shown in Figure 4-18.

Comments

Additional harmonics can be added to the motions of the letter elements to make them do odd phased accordion, stacking poker chip, polka silliness. For example, substituting the *Y1-Y8* variables with ones having an extra trig function, like

```
define major 0.2
define minor 0.05
define Y2 1*spacing*major*sin(frame*24*rad) + 1*minor*sin(frame*48*rad)
```

adds a little extra hop to every bounce. You can also precess each letter component like a top, and make them belly dance. There's enough extra detail in that one to cover it in the next section.

continued from previous page

```
                    tx = tx * 1.04      ' move the middle two control point sets
                    tz = tz * 1.04      ' out to make the spiral rounder
                END IF
                CIRCLE (tx, ty), .1, a + k
            NEXT a

            ' ang isn't indexed after the last set,
            ' so the Bezier ends will overlap

            IF n < 4 THEN ang = ang + (45 / 3)
        NEXT n
    NEXT patch
NEXT dat

SUB rotate (x, y, z)

'rotate

    x0 = x
    y0 = y
    z0 = z

    x1 = x0
    y1 = y0 * COS(xrotate * rad) - z0 * SIN(xrotate * rad)
    z1 = y0 * SIN(xrotate * rad) + z0 * COS(xrotate * rad)

    x2 = z1 * SIN(yrotate * rad) + x1 * COS(yrotate * rad)
    y2 = y1
    z2 = z1 * COS(yrotate * rad) - x1 * SIN(yrotate * rad)

    x3 = x2 * COS(zrotate * rad) - y2 * SIN(zrotate * rad)
    y3 = x2 * SIN(zrotate * rad) + y2 * COS(zrotate * rad)
    z3 = z2

    x = x3
    y = y3
    z = z3

END SUB
```

Polyray Code

The Polyray code for the animation is broken into two parts. The first part sets the scene and generates the motion; the second defines the object being moved. The first part is easy.

```
// Spiraling Bezier Animation: Jeff Bowermaster

start_frame 0
end_frame 44
total_frames 45
```

```
define index 360/total_frames

outfile thred

include "\PLY\COLORS.INC"

// set up background color & lights
background midnightblue
light <0,25,0>
light <10,50,-120>

viewpoint {
    from <5.01, 40.01,-40.01>
    at  <0,0,7.5>
    up   <0, 1,  0>
    angle 30
    resolution 320,200
    aspect 1.433
    }

// make a tabletop
define table
object {
    polygon 4,<-25,0.01,-25>,<25,0.01,-25>,<25,0.01,25>,<-25,0.01,25>
    reflective_blue
}
object {
    box <-25,-1,-25>,<25,0,25>
    texture {surface { color navyblue ambient 0.2 diffuse 0.6}}
}

define pi 3.14159
define rad pi/180

// blobs 3-phased height components - each 1/3 out from the other
define a 7 + 3*sin(index*frame*rad)
define b 7 + 3*sin(index*(frame+(total_frames/3)*rad))
define c 7 + 3*sin(index*(frame+(2*total_frames/3)*rad))

object {
    blob 0.6:
        sphere <0,a,0>, 3, 3,
        sphere <0,b,0>, 4, 4,
        sphere <0,c,0>, 5, 5
    reflective_cyan
}

// rotate the base Bezier patch
define p1 rotate(<1,1,0>,<0,0,frame*index/2>)
define p2 rotate(<-1,1,0>,<0,0,frame*index/2>)
define p3 rotate(<1,-1,0>,<0,0,frame*index/2>)
define p4 rotate(<-1,-1,0>,<0,0,frame*index/2>)
```

continued on next page

continued from previous page

```
// bottom
define t09   [v05,v06,v11]
define t10   [v06,v02,v11]
define t11   [v02,v01,v11]
define t12   [v01,v05,v11]

// top
define t13   [v07,v08,v12]
define t14   [v08,v04,v12]
define t15   [v04,v03,v12]
define t16   [v03,v07,v12]

// left
define t17   [v08,v05,v13]
define t18   [v05,v01,v13]
define t19   [v01,v04,v13]
define t20   [v04,v08,v13]

// right
define t21   [v06,v07,v14]
define t22   [v07,v03,v14]
define t23   [v03,v02,v14]
define t24   [v02,v06,v14]

object {
   object { polygon 3, t01[0], t01[1], t01[2] } +
   object { polygon 3, t02[0], t02[1], t02[2] } +
   object { polygon 3, t03[0], t03[1], t03[2] } +
   object { polygon 3, t04[0], t04[1], t04[2] } +
   object { polygon 3, t05[0], t05[1], t05[2] } +
   object { polygon 3, t06[0], t06[1], t06[2] } +
   object { polygon 3, t07[0], t07[1], t07[2] } +
   object { polygon 3, t08[0], t08[1], t08[2] } +
   object { polygon 3, t09[0], t09[1], t09[2] } +
   object { polygon 3, t10[0], t10[1], t10[2] } +
   object { polygon 3, t11[0], t11[1], t11[2] } +
   object { polygon 3, t12[0], t12[1], t12[2] } +
   object { polygon 3, t13[0], t13[1], t13[2] } +
   object { polygon 3, t14[0], t14[1], t14[2] } +
   object { polygon 3, t15[0], t15[1], t15[2] } +
   object { polygon 3, t16[0], t16[1], t16[2] } +
   object { polygon 3, t17[0], t17[1], t17[2] } +
   object { polygon 3, t18[0], t18[1], t18[2] } +
   object { polygon 3, t19[0], t19[1], t19[2] } +
   object { polygon 3, t20[0], t20[1], t20[2] } +
   object { polygon 3, t21[0], t21[1], t21[2] } +
   object { polygon 3, t22[0], t22[1], t22[2] } +
   object { polygon 3, t23[0], t23[1], t23[2] } +
   object { polygon 3, t24[0], t24[1], t24[2] }

   texture {
      checker matte_magenta, matte_orange
      translate <0, -0.1, 0>
      scale <0.2, 0.2, 0.2>
```

```
     }
    rotate <xrotate, yrotate, zrotate>
}

object {
  sphere <0, 0, 0>, 9
  chrome
    }

object {
  sphere <0, 0, 0>, 1.2
  chrome
    }
```

The object is defined as 24 triangular patches in vector notation. It's actually just a way of keeping point locations tidy. For example, the first triangle is defined as three points:

```
define t01   [v01,v02,v09]
```

This definition is subsequently used to define the polygon using the matrix notation:

```
object { polygon 3, t01[0], t01[1], t01[2] }
```

The substitution here is v01 = t01[0], v02 = t01[1], and v09 = t01[2], but it could just as easily have been done with

```
object { polygon 3, v01, v02, v09 }
```

The difference is cosmetic. We've spruced up the model a bit by placing the object between two concentric mirrored spheres. The inner one shows how we're moving the cube back and forth, and the outer one reflects the scene back to the inner one, producing the illusion that the cube is hollow. The motion is however the same as our stick figure cube. A sample frame is shown in Figure 4-27.

Figure 4-27 Box in between concentric mirrored spheres

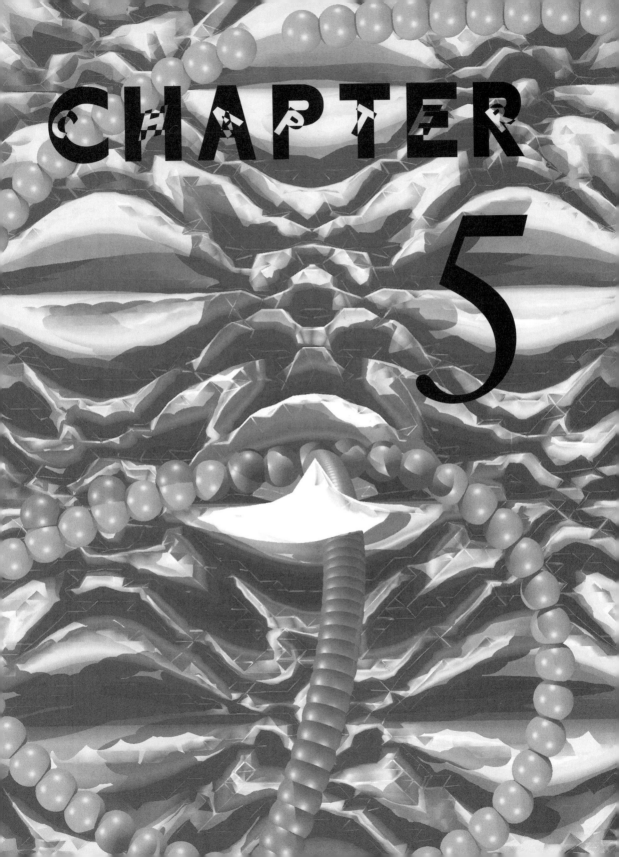

CHAPTER

5

5

PARTICLE SYSTEMS

Particle system animations are different from the kind of systems we've dealt with so far, since rather than directly controlling the shapes or motions of objects in a scene, you define rules which govern how objects move and the shapes they assume. In a sense, it's very similar to the classic cellular automata program LIFE. In LIFE, you define rules for cell propagation and some initial conditions and then sit back and watch little pixel colonies grow and retreat, evolve and develop, controlled by the rules you selected.

continued from previous page

```
    pi = 3.14159
    rad = pi / 180

    n = 0
    damp = 2.4     ' damping
    a = -.01       ' acceleration

    d = 1 - 10 ^ -damp

    ' initial positions
    FOR b = 1 TO 5
       READ offx(b)
       rx(b) = offx(b)
       x(b) = offx(b)
    NEXT b
    DATA -4,-2, 0,2,4

    ' initial velocities
    FOR b = 1 TO 5
       READ v(b)
       rv(b) = v(b)
    NEXT b
    DATA   .0,.0,.0,.0,.5


    ' embrace conditional setup

    FOR b = 1 TO 5
       FOR c = 1 TO 5
          embr(b, c) = 0
       NEXT c
    NEXT b

DO WHILE INKEY$ = ""

    ' move all the objects
    FOR b = 1 TO 5
       x(b) = x(b) + v(b)
    NEXT b

    FOR b = 1 TO 5
       FOR c = 1 TO 5

          ' distance between any two balls
          d(b, c) = ((x(b) - x(c)) ^ 2) ^ .5

          ' if two balls hit, swap their velocities
          IF d(b, c)<1 AND d(b, c)>0 AND embr(b, c)=0 AND embr(c, d)=0 THEN
                temp = v(b)
                v(b) = v(c)
                v(c) = temp
                embr(b, c) = 1
                embr(c, b) = 1
          END IF
```

```
      ' embr prevents oscillating collisions;
      ' the balls must come apart before checking to see if
      ' they're close enough to swap velocities again

      IF d(b, c)>1 AND d(c, b)>1 AND embr(b, c)=1 AND embr(c, b)=1 THEN
         embr(b, c) = 0
         embr(c, b) = 0
      END IF

   NEXT c
   NEXT b

   FOR b = 1 TO 5
      ' velocity = velocity + acceleration, centered on the offset
      v(b) = (v(b) + a * (x(b) - offx(b))) * d
   NEXT b

   FOR b = 1 TO 5
      ' fake a pendulum
      cy(b) = .07 * (rx(b) - x(b)) ^ 2

      LINE (rx(b), 8)-(ox(b), ocy(b)), 0    ' undraw the current screen
      CIRCLE (ox(b), ocy(b)), .5, 0         ' (draw in color 0 = black)
      LINE (rx(b), 8)-(x(b), cy(b)), 15     ' draw the current screen
      CIRCLE (x(b), cy(b)), .5, 15          ' (draw in color 15 = white)
      ox(b) = x(b)                          ' save the current screen
      oy(b) = Y(b)                          ' variables (ox=old-x; oy=old-y)
      ocy(b) = cy(b)
   NEXT b
LOOP
```

How It Works

We establish the initial positions $x(b)$ and velocities $v(b)$ for our pendulums, specify values for acceleration and damping, and set our animation into motion by incrementing each object's location by its velocity. During each pass, a collision is looked for and acted upon on the basis of two factors:

- Are two spheres close enough to have collided?

- Is this the first time this condition has been true recently?

Once a collision has been detected, we swap the velocities of the objects. A problem with this approach is that if their rebound doesn't completely separate them by the next pass, we'll turn right around and swap their velocities again, resulting in an oscillatory embrace. We prevent this by using the variable *embr* as a toggle. Once two objects collide, they must come completely apart for at least one cycle before we check for another collision.

continued from previous page

```
      'position = position + velocity
      x(b) = x(b) + vx(b)
      y(b) = y(b) + vy(b)
      z(b) = z(b) + vz(b)

  NEXT b

  FOR b = 1 TO bls

   ' velocity = velocity + acceleration, centered on the offset
   vx(b) = (vx(b) + accel * SGN(x(b) - offx(b))) * damp
   vy(b) = (vy(b) + accel * SGN(y(b) - offy(b))) * damp
   vz(b) = (vz(b) + accel * SGN(z(b) - offz(b))) * damp

   FOR c = 1 TO bls

        'distance between any two balls
        d(b, c) = ((x(b)-x(c))^ 2 + (y(b)-y(c))^ 2 + (z(b)-z(c))^ 2) ^ .5

        ' if two balls hit, swap their velocities
        IF d(b, c) < dist AND embr(b, c) = 0 AND embr(c, b) = 0 THEN

           temp = vx(b)
           vx(b) = vx(c)
           vx(c) = temp

           temp = vy(b)
           vy(b) = vy(c)
           vy(c) = temp

           temp = vz(b)
           vz(b) = vz(c)
           vz(c) = temp

           embr(b, c) = 1
           embr(c, b) = 1

        END IF

        ' embr prevents oscillating collisions:
        ' the balls must first come back apart before checking to see if
        ' they're close enough to swap their velocities again

   IF d(b, c)>dist AND d(c, b)>dist AND embr(b, c)=1 AND embr(c, b)=1 THEN
      embr(b, c) = 0
      embr(c, b) = 0
   END IF

   NEXT c
   CIRCLE (ox(b), oy(b)), dist / 2, 0
   CIRCLE (x(b), y(b)), dist / 2, 12

   ' if you want to see the other axes...
```

```
   'CIRCLE (ox(b), oz(b)), dist / 2, 0
   'CIRCLE (x(b), z(b)), dist / 2, 13

   'CIRCLE (oy(b), oz(b)), dist / 2, 0
   'CIRCLE (y(b), z(b)), dist / 2, 14

   ox(b) = x(b)
   oy(b) = y(b)
   oz(b) = z(b)

   NEXT b

   n = n + 1
   damp = .85 + .5 * SIN(n / 2)
LOOP
```

How It Works

BUMPZ.BAS extends the example in Section 5.1 to three dimensions, treating the positions and velocities separately for the *x, y,* and *z* axes. Arrays hold values for the control variables for each ball. An initial scattering of balls is generated using a random function, but each new ball is checked to see if it already overlaps one in the field, and if it does, another attempt is made.

The motion of all the balls is towards the origin, set by the variables *offx, offy,* and *offz.* We made this an array, one for each ball, so that we could create "mixed fruit vibrating in jello" sort of animation by setting the attractor for each ball to its original position if we want. It was set here to attract all balls to <0,0,0>, but try replacing the zeros with the variables and see what you think.

We display only one view for the coordinates, the *x-y* plane. We can display the *y-z* and *x-z* plane views as well by uncommenting those lines.

The damping is periodically turned up and down using

```
damp = 0.85 + 0.5 * SIN(n / 2)
```

causing it to vary from between 0.35 to 1.35, so that it periodically becomes a gain term, accelerating the motion rather than slowing it.

Polyray Code

One feature that is tough to do inside Polyray is collision detection. Without loops, the only way to check for collisions in Polyray involves writing roughly n^2 IF statements, where *n* is the number of items. In this case, 9 items would require 81 IF statements. As fun as this might sound, we'll omit it in the Polyray code.

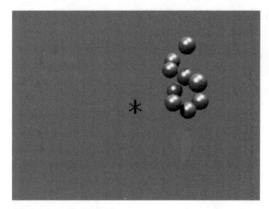

Figure 5-2 Sloshing spheres

The following Polyray code excerpt orbits nine shiny yellow spheres around the origin and modulates all their speeds in a concerted fashion (Figure 5-2).

```
// Orbitals - Particle Systems

start_frame 0
end_frame 999
total_frames 1000

outfile plnet

include "\PLY\COLORS.INC"

viewpoint {
   from <25,25,-25>
   at <0,0,0>
   up <0,1,0>
   angle 30
   resolution 160,120
   aspect 1.43
   }
background SkyBlue

light white, <-5,100,-50>
light white, < 5,100, 50>

define dist 0.5
define speed 0.01
define accel -0.04
define damp  1 + 0.5 * SIN(frame / 2)

if (frame == start_frame) {
   // set the initial conditions
```

```
   static define bx1 3.16102
   static define by1 7.35870
   static define bz1 5.285980
   static define vx1 -0.00150
   static define vy1 -0.00456
   static define vz1 -0.00410

   static define bx2 0.16661
   static define by2 3.83032
   static define bz2 6.53091
   static define vx2 -0.00156
   static define vy2 -0.00293
   static define vz2  0.00036
...
  }
else {
   static define bx1 bx1 + vx1
   static define bx2 bx2 + vx2
   static define bx3 bx3 + vx3
   static define bx4 bx4 + vx4
   static define bx5 bx5 + vx5
   static define bx6 bx6 + vx6
   static define bx7 bx7 + vx7
   static define bx8 bx8 + vx8
   static define bx9 bx9 + vx9

   static define by1 by1 + vy1
   static define by2 by2 + vy2
   static define by3 by3 + vy3
...
}

// velocity = velocity + acceleration, centered on the origin


if (bx1>0) { static define vx1 vx1 + accel*damp } else { static define vx1 vx1 ⇐
- accel*damp }
if (by1>0) { static define vy1 vy1 + accel*damp } else { static define vy1 vy1 ⇐
- accel*damp }
if (bz1>0) { static define vz1 vz1 + accel*damp } else { static define vz1 vz1 ⇐
- accel*damp }

if (bx2>0) { static define vx2 vx2 + accel*damp } else { static define vx2 vx2 ⇐
- accel*damp }
if (by2>0) { static define vy2 vy2 + accel*damp } else { static define vy2 vy2 ⇐
- accel*damp }
if (bz2>0) { static define vz2 vz2 + accel*damp } else { static define vz2 vz2 ⇐
- accel*damp }

if (bx3>0) { static define vx3 vx3 + accel*damp } else { static define vx3 vx3 ⇐
- accel*damp }
```

continued on next page

continued from previous page

```
define a13   a01*0.9
define b13   b01*0.9
define c13   c01*0.9

define a14   a02*0.9
define b14   b02*0.9
define c14   c02*0.9

define a15   a03*0.9
define b15   b03*0.9
define c15   c03*0.9

define a16   a04*0.9
define b16   b04*0.9
define c16   c04*0.9
...


include "col.inc"

define d01 (a01+b01+c01)/3
define e01 < sin(01)*fr*rspeed,sin(01+2)*fr*rspeed,sin(01+2)*fr*rspeed>
define f01 < sin(01)*fr*lspeed,sin(01+2)*fr*lspeed,sin(01+2)*fr*lspeed>
define t01 object { polygon 3, a01, b01, c01 translate -d01 rotate e01
translate d01+f01 refl_01}

define d02 (a02+b02+c02)/3
define e02 < sin(02)*fr*rspeed,sin(02+2)*fr*rspeed,sin(02+2)*fr*rspeed>
define f02 < sin(02)*fr*lspeed,sin(02+2)*fr*lspeed,sin(02+2)*fr*lspeed>
define t02 object { polygon 3, a02, b02, c02 translate -d02 rotate e02
translate d02+f02 refl_02}

define d03 (a03+b03+c03)/3
define e03 < sin(03)*fr*rspeed,sin(03+2)*fr*rspeed,sin(03+2)*fr*rspeed>
define f03 < sin(03)*fr*lspeed,sin(03+2)*fr*lspeed,sin(03+2)*fr*lspeed>
define t03 object { polygon 3, a03, b03, c03 translate -d03 rotate e03
translate d03+f03 refl_03}

define d04 (a04+b04+c04)/3
define e04 < sin(04)*fr*rspeed,sin(04+2)*fr*rspeed,sin(04+2)*fr*rspeed>
define f04 < sin(04)*fr*lspeed,sin(04+2)*fr*lspeed,sin(04+2)*fr*lspeed>
define t04 object { polygon 3, a04, b04, c04 translate -d04 rotate e04
translate d04+f04 refl_04}
...


// Polyray's parser doesn't care if you call one item per line
// or all at once.  These are the triangle objects

    t01 t02 t03 t04 t05 t06 t07 t08 t09 t10 t11 t12
    t13 t14 t15 t16 t17 t18 t19 t20 t21 t22 t23 t24

// set up background color & lights
background midnightblue
```

```
light <0,15,-12>
light <12,-15,-12>
light <2,2,2>,<0,0,0>

define bumpy_yellow
texture {
   special surface {
      color <1.5,0.8,0>
      normal N + (dnoise(3*W) - white/2)
      ambient 0.2
      diffuse 0.3
      specular white, 0.7
      microfacet Cook 5
      }
   scale <0.05, 0.05, 0.05>
   }

object {sphere <-10,  0,  0>,0.4 translate <frame/2,0,0> bumpy_yellow}
object {sphere <  0,-10,  0>,0.4 translate <0,frame/2,0> bumpy_yellow}
object {sphere <  0,  0,-10>,0.4 translate <0,0,frame/2> bumpy_yellow}
object {sphere < 10,  0,  0>,0.4 translate <-frame/2,0,0> bumpy_yellow}
object {sphere <  0, 10,  0>,0.4 translate <0,-frame/2,0> bumpy_yellow}
object {sphere <  0,  0, 10>,0.4 translate <0,0,-frame/2> bumpy_yellow}

viewpoint {
   from <6, 12,-8>
   at <0,0,0>
   up   <0, 1,  0>
   angle 30
   resolution 80,50
   aspect 1.43
   }
```

How It Works

This abbreviated listing for SHATTER.PI shows the definitions of the triangles (big and little) and the triangle dispersal control code which sends our triangles flying off. We create a bumpy yellow texture, and apply it to six spheres symmetrically arranged around the origin. They all approach the origin simultaneously and collide with the box at frame 20. We've multiplied both the rotational speed and the leaving speed of the triangles by the frame counter

```
define rspeed frame*0.1
define lspeed frame*0.001
```

so both elements accelerate as the animation progresses. Scaling them by 0.1 and 0.001 coordinates the motions, making the box fly apart just as the balls arrive to smash it.

continued from previous page
```
define refl_001 texture { reflective { color <0.71073, 0.49529, 0.85240 > } }
define refl_002 texture { reflective { color <0.35038, 0.02182, 0.08978 > } }
define refl_003 texture { reflective { color <0.51111, 0.37768, 0.93539 > } }
...
...

// dispersal code

define d001 (a001+b001+c001)/3
define e001 < sin(  1)*fr*rspeed,sin(  1+1)*fr*rspeed,sin(  1+2)*fr*rspeed>
define f001 < sin(  1)*fr*lspeed,sin(  1+1)*fr*lspeed,sin(  1+2)*fr*lspeed>
object { polygon 3, a001, b001, c001 translate -d001 rotate e001 translate ⇐
d001+f001 refl_001 }

define d002 (a002+b002+c002)/3
define e002 < sin(  2)*fr*rspeed,sin(  2+1)*fr*rspeed,sin(  2+2)*fr*rspeed>
define f002 < sin(  2)*fr*lspeed,sin(  2+1)*fr*lspeed,sin(  2+2)*fr*lspeed>
object { polygon 3, a002, b002, c002 translate -d002 rotate e002 translate ⇐
d002+f002 refl_002 }

define d003 (a003+b003+c003)/3
define e003 < sin(  3)*fr*rspeed,sin(  3+1)*fr*rspeed,sin(  3+2)*fr*rspeed>
define f003 < sin(  3)*fr*lspeed,sin(  3+1)*fr*lspeed,sin(  3+2)*fr*lspeed>
object { polygon 3, a003, b003, c003 translate -d003 rotate e003 translate ⇐
d003+f003 refl_003 }
...
...
```

How It Works

We decided to start here with a shattered blob, bring it back together, then fly it apart again. Looking at the dispersion code above, the variable *fr* controls the amount of scattering. When *fr* = 0, we have our fully assembled object. Any value other than zero leads to a dismantled object. We'll use a 180 frame animation, and the following statement.

```
define fr frame - 90
```

This line means that at frame 0, *fr* = -90 and our blob is shattered out of view. It assembles itself at frame 90, (where *fr* = 0) and flies apart again by frame 180 (*fr* = 90). The variables *lspeed* and *rspeed* scale how far *fr* = -90 takes us out, and the rate of rotation of the pieces as they come and go. It's shown flying apart in Figure 5-5.

Comments

One of the problems dealing with files like these (this one's over 400K) is how long it takes to load into an editor. Sometimes all you want to do is adjust something small like the viewpoint or the lighting. It's easier to split

Figure 5-5 Shattering blob

this file in two, creating a small control file containing just the viewpoint, lights, and constants (SHATBLB.PI) and a large data file (FRAGBLOB.INC), which contains the traingles, the textures and the motion code. This larger file is included in the control file using the line

```
include "fragblob.inc"
```

Another problem you'll encounter with files of this size is long preprocessing time (over a minute per frame for this file). In developing control structures for your own animations, you may want to reduce the item count to under 100 during development, which will preprocess quickly and allow you to adjust the motion to suit you. Once you're happy, then increase it to the full count for the final render.

5.5 How do I...
Give a salt crystal indigestion?

You'll find the code for this in: PLY\CHAPTER5\TUG

Problem

Let's say you have a cubical crystal lattice and you'd like to make it appear that something was crawling around inside it, forcing the lattice to bulge out and distort as a result of this internal perturbation. Once the disturbance passed, the lattice would return to its original form. This effect can be created by defining the position and radius of the spheres in the lattice to vary depending on how close they are to repellers orbiting freely throughout the structure.

Technique

Crystalline structures are highly ordered collections of objects in 3-D space. This animation starts with such a structure, a six by six by six array of spheres. Small light sources orbit this array and perturb both the positions and (later on) the diameters of the spheres proportionally to their distance from the spheres (see Figure 5-6).

Since light sources are invisible in ray tracers, we've placed spheres around them to make them visible. We turn off their shadows so the light can get through. Discs surrounding our structure will catch the shadows as both the lights move around and the entire shape changes structure. We'll place the camera on an orbital platform and circle the structure for a complete view of the proceedings.

How It Works

Rather than give the animation code first and then explain how it works, we're going to cover what's being done first, and then detail how certain effects were achieved.

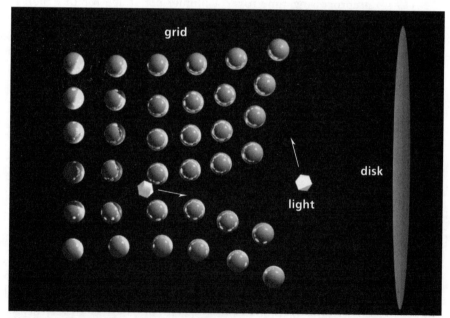

Figure 5-6 Orbital repellers perturb a six by six grid

The orbital lights are the central controlling elements in this animation. They are placed into circular motions using sines and cosines, and offset using constants and phases:

```
define ph1 0*pi/3
define ph2 2*pi/3
define ph3 4*pi/3

// three little orbital repellers

define   fx1   2.5 + 5 * COS(angle_nor+ph1)
define   fy1   2.5 + 5 * SIN(angle_nor+ph1)
define   fz1   2.5

define   fx2   2.5 + 5 * COS(angle_nor+ph2)
define   fy2   2.5
define   fz2   2.5 + 5 * SIN(angle_nor+ph2)

define   fx3   2.5
define   fy3   2.5 + 5 * COS(angle_nor+ph3)
define   fz3   2.5 + 5 * SIN(angle_nor+ph3)
```

The grid is built using QuickBasic code. The positions of every object must allow these orbital elements to influence their position and size. The variables *a, b,* and *c* are the array counters for the grid, and also the positions of the grid elements when they're at rest. The first element (0,0,0) is defined using the following lines

```
define a 00
define b 00
define c 00

include "tug.inc"

define x000000 a + f1 * drx1 + f2 * drx2 + f3 * drx3
define y000000 b + f1 * dry1 + f2 * dry2 + f3 * dry3
define z000000 c + f1 * drz1 + f2 * drz2 + f3 * drz3

object { sphere <x000000,y000000,z000000>,0.2 reflective_white }
```

The TUG.INC file generates the factors, based on where the orbital lights are, that shift the positions of the elements in the grid. This code is used for each sphere in the grid. With 216 objects, making it a single include file saved a lot of disk space. The repeated file TUG.INC contains the following code:

```
define d1   ((a - fx1) ^ 2 + (b - fy1) ^ 2 + (c - fz1) ^ 2) ^ 0.5
define d2   ((a - fx2) ^ 2 + (b - fy2) ^ 2 + (c - fz2) ^ 2) ^ 0.5
define d3   ((a - fx3) ^ 2 + (b - fy3) ^ 2 + (c - fz3) ^ 2) ^ 0.5

define drx1   a - fx1
```

continued on next page

continued from previous page

```
define ph2 2*pi/3
define ph3 4*pi/3

// little orbital repellers
define orbit 2

define fx1  3 + orbit * COS(angle_nor * 4 + ph1)
define fy1  3 + 1.5 * COS(angle_nor) + orbit * SIN(angle_nor * 4 + ph1)
define fz1  3

define fx2  3 + 1.5 * COS(angle_nor) + orbit * COS(angle_nor * 4 + ph2)
define fy2  3
define fz2  3 + orbit * SIN(angle_nor * 4 + ph2)

define fx3  3
define fy3  3 + orbit * COS(angle_nor * 4 + ph3)
define fz3  3 + 1.5 * COS(angle_nor) + orbit * SIN(angle_nor * 4 + ph3)

// UNUSED 4th repeller
define fx4  0
define fy4  0
define fz4  0

define  f  1
define  p  2

object {
   sphere <fx1,fy1,fz1>,0.2
   shading_flags 32 + 8 + 4 + 2 +1
   shiny_yellow
}

object {
   sphere <fx2,fy2,fz2>,0.2
   shading_flags 32 + 8 + 4 + 2 +1
   shiny_blue
}

object {
   sphere <fx3,fy3,fz3>,0.2
   shading_flags 32 + 8 + 4 + 2 +1
   shiny_red
}

light <0.8,0.8,0>, <fx1,fy1,fz1>
light <0,0,0.8>, <fx2,fy2,fz2>
light <0.8,0,0>, <fx3,fy3,fz3>

light white*0.25, <9,15,-10>

object { disc <-20,0,0>,<1,0,0>, 20 matte_white }
object { disc <0,-20,0>,<0,1,0>, 20 matte_white }
```

```
object { disc <0,0, 20>,<0,0,1>, 20 matte_white }

object { disc <20,0,0>,<1,0,0>, 20 matte_white }
object { disc <0,20,0>,<0,1,0>, 20 matte_white }
object { disc <0,0,-20>,<0,0,1>, 20 matte_white }
```

Main Loop

As with all animations involving several hundred objects, we automate the creation of the 216 elements programmatically. In this particular case, we can also place repetitive code in an include file, call it as needed, and reduce the file size:

```
PRINT #1, "//main loop"
PRINT #1,

FOR a = 0 TO 5
FOR b = 0 TO 5
FOR c = 0 TO 5

a$ = RIGHT$("00" + LTRIM$(STR$(a)), 2)
b$ = RIGHT$("00" + LTRIM$(STR$(b)), 2)
c$ = RIGHT$("00" + LTRIM$(STR$(c)), 2)
x$ = "x" + a$ + b$ + c$
y$ = "y" + a$ + b$ + c$
z$ = "z" + a$ + b$ + c$

PRINT #1, "define a "; a$
PRINT #1, "define b "; b$
PRINT #1, "define c "; c$
PRINT #1,
PRINT #1, "include "; CHR$(34); "tug.inc"; CHR$(34)
PRINT #1,
PRINT #1, "define "; x$; " a + f1 * drx1 + f2 * drx2 + f3 * drx3"
PRINT #1, "define "; y$; " b + f1 * dry1 + f2 * dry2 + f3 * dry3"
PRINT #1, "define "; z$; " c + f1 * drz1 + f2 * drz2 + f3 * drz3"
PRINT #1,
PRINT #1, USING "object { sphere <\      \,\      \,\      \>,0.2+f1+f2+f3
reflective__white }"; x$, y$, z$

NEXT c
NEXT b
NEXT a
```

We convert the variables *a*, *b*, and *c* to strings, join them together to create our position control variable names, and then loop through and automatically create all the control code for the objects. This process could be extended to generate thousands of elements, although we'd eventually run out of memory and the patience to render such a scene.

continued from previous page

```
PRINT #1,
NEXT x
NEXT y


FOR x = 0 TO 59

   READ clr$

   PRINT #1, "object {"
   PRINT #1, "   blob min:"

   FOR y = 0 TO 3

      counta$ = RIGHT$("00" + LTRIM$(STR$(y)), 2)
      countb$ = RIGHT$("00" + LTRIM$(STR$(x)), 2)
      countc$ = counta$ + countb$

      Vx$ = "< Vx" + countc$ + ", "
      Vy$ = " Vy" + countc$ + ", "
      Vz$ = " Vz" + countc$ + " >"

      V$ = Vx$ + Vy$ + Vz$
      PRINT #1, USING "      str, radius, \                    \,"; V$
   NEXT y

   counta$ = "04"
   countb$ = RIGHT$("00" + LTRIM$(STR$(x)), 2)
   countc$ = counta$ + countb$

   Vx$ = "< Vx" + countc$ + ", "
   Vy$ = " Vy" + countc$ + ", "
   Vz$ = " Vz" + countc$ + " >"

   V$ = Vx$ + Vy$ + Vz$

   PRINT #1, USING "      str, radius, \                    \"; V$
   PRINT #1, "     u_steps 20"
   PRINT #1, "     v_steps 20"
   PRINT #1, "     texture {"
   PRINT #1, "        surface {"
   PRINT #1, "           ambient "; clr$; ", 0.2"
   PRINT #1, "           diffuse "; clr$; ", 0.5"
   PRINT #1, "           specular white, 0.7"
   PRINT #1, "        }"
   PRINT #1, "        rotate <0,0,0>"
   PRINT #1, "     }"
   PRINT #1, "}"
   PRINT #1,
NEXT x

CLOSE #1
```

```
kolors:

DATA "Aquamarine"
DATA "BlueViolet"
DATA "Brown"
DATA "CadetBlue"
...
```

This program creates SWARM.PI the following Polyray data file, abbreviated here to save space:

```
//
// SWARM.PI
//
// Polyray input file - Jeff Bowermaster
// Based on Eric Deren's MERGE2

start_frame      0
end_frame     3500
total_frames 3501
outfile "swrm"

define min 2.0
define str 4.0
define radius 15.0
define u 20
define v 20

// set up the camera
viewpoint {
   from <0,100,-225>
   at  <0,0,0>
   up  <0,1,0>
   angle 45
   resolution 160,120
   aspect 1.333
   }

// set up background color & lights
background skyblue
light  < 220,240,-800>
light  < 420,240,-800>

include "\PLY\COLORS.INC"

define ampl 45

define a00 (frame+ 0 )/33.333333
define a01 (frame+ 1 )/33.333333
define a02 (frame+ 2 )/33.333333
define a03 (frame+ 3 )/33.333333
define a04 (frame+ 4 )/33.333333
```

continued on next page

continued from previous page
```
PRINT #1,
NEXT item

CLOSE #1
```

How It Works

PRINT statements are used to create a canned heading for our Polyray code so that we don't have to deal with it. Then we enter a loop that defines 500 spherical particles, each moving independently. The control code for every particle is identical, but we use the random Brownian function to give each particle its own path. An example of this control code for one particle follows:

```
// set the initial conditions
if (frame == start_frame) {
    static define x000 0
    static define y000 0
    static define z000 0
    define r000 [5*brownian(<0.1,0.1,0.1>)]
    define radius r000[0][0]
    define theta  360 * r000[0][1] * rad
    define phi    (30 + 30 * r000[0][2]) * rad
    define velo r000[0][0]
    static define vx000 radius * sin(phi) * cos(theta)
    static define vy000 radius * cos(phi) + velo
    static define vz000 radius * sin(phi) * sin(theta)
}
else {
    static define x000 x000 + vx000
    static define y000 y000 + vy000
    static define z000 z000 + vz000
}

static define vy000 vy000 - g
define dist (x000^2 +z000^2)^0.5
define ring dist/run
if (y000 + ring*rise-br < 0)
    { static define vy000 fabs(vy000)*damp
}
object { sphere <x000,y000,z000>,0.5 shiny_coral }
```

Each particle is given an initial position, and then a random number between zero and one generated by the Brownian function sets the initial velocity for that particle in polar coordinate notation:

```
x = r*sin(phi)cos(theta)
y = r*cos(phi)
z = r*sin(phi)sin(theta)
```

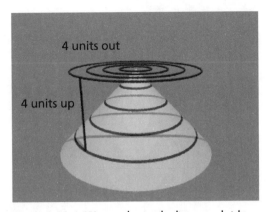

Figure 5-16 A 45° cone, showing the distance vs. height relationship

Use polar coordinates rather than Cartesian notation to effect a spherical eruption. Cartesian coordinates would result in cubical eruptions. Polar coordinates define locations by two angles (*phi* and *theta*) and a distance from the origin (x). All particles are given a random upward velocity *velo*, which adds to the one specified with the polar coordinates. The gravity variable g eventually overcomes this upward motion, and changing g is a convenient means of handling the overall size of the eruption.

After the first frame, the positions of the particles are simply indexed by their velocity. The upward velocity slows under the force of gravity:

```
static define vy000 vy000 - g
```

and then we deal with the cone. We defined a white 45° cone for our mountain. The important thing to note about 45° cones is that the distance out from the center (the radius) will always equal the absolute value of the height, provided the tip is placed at the origin, like this one is (Figure 5-16).

Figure 5-17 Erupting malted milk ball volcano

In the development phase of this animation, a set of rings was used which extend downwards from the eruption point to define a staircase which the balls bounced down. Making those steps finer and finer eventually gave a cone. Whenever the particles y coordinate (which is negative) tries to penetrate this cone, making `y000 + ring*rise-br < 0`, its velocity flips. In other words, we make it bounce. A frame during the eruption is shown in Figure 5-17.

CHAPTER

6

continued from previous page

```
FOR y = 1 TO 4
    FOR x = 1 TO 4
        colornum = x + ((y - 1) * 4) - 1
        READ red(colornum), green(colornum), blue(colornum)
        KOLOR = 65536 * blue(colornum) + 256 * green(colornum) + red(colornum)
        PALETTE colornum, KOLOR
        COLOR colornum
    NEXT x
NEXT y


'rainbow palette

DATA  0,  0,  0
DATA 32,  0,  0
DATA 42,  0,  0
DATA 58, 16,  0
DATA 63, 32,  0
DATA 58, 56,  0
DATA 16, 42,  0
DATA  0, 30, 36
DATA  0, 20, 40
DATA  0, 10, 48
DATA  0,  0, 63
DATA 20,  0, 53
DATA 23,  0, 29
DATA 19,  7, 17
DATA 50, 40, 45
DATA 63, 63, 63

pi = 3.1415926535#
rad = pi / 180

'= MODIFY THIS LINE SO THE BATCH FILE ENDS UP IN YOUR Polyray Directory =

OPEN "bbanim.bat" FOR OUTPUT AS #1     'batch file to run the
                                       'animations

FOR frame = 0 TO 358 STEP 2

'=======================================================================

'make a unit pentagram

i = 1

FOR a = frame + 144 TO frame + 432 STEP 72     ' odd phase makes 1 & 2
                                               ' parallel parallel to x-axis
    x = SIN(a * rad) / 1.1755695#  ' the 'unit' part
    y = COS(a * rad) / 1.1755695#  ' space each member 1 unit apart
    penta(i).x = x
    penta(i).y = y
    penta(i).z = 0
    i = i + 1
NEXT a
```

How It Works

The last section set the palette and defined our first pentagram. The next section will take each side of this pentagram and attach a hexagram to it so that both shapes share two vertices. Actually only two points of the pentagram are used, as they're positioned conveniently with respect to the origin to exploit the symmetry.

We use the nomenclature

hex(a,b), where *a* represents a particular hexagram,
and *b* represents a particular sphere within that hexagram.
So hex (1,2) is the second sphere in the first hexagram.

Start with the *b=2* sphere, translate it to the origin, dragging the *b=1* sphere along with it, rotate *b=1* 240° about *b=2*, then translate *b=2* (+baggage) back to its original position. Repeat with *b=3*, rotating *b=2*, (then 4,3 and 5,4) leapfrogging a hex into shape:

```
xrotate = 0
yrotate = 0
zrotate = 240

' make hex elements 1 & 2 two sides vertices of the pentagram

  FOR b = 1 TO 2
    hex(1, b) = penta(b)
  NEXT b

  a = 1

  FOR b = 3 TO 6

'translate

    hex(a, b).x = hex(a, b - 2).x - hex(a, b - 1).x
    hex(a, b).y = hex(a, b - 2).y - hex(a, b - 1).y
    hex(a, b).z = hex(a, b - 2).z - hex(a, b - 1).z

'rotate

CALL rotate (hex(a,b).x, hex(a,b).y, hex(a,b).z)

'translate back

    hex(a, b).x = hex(a, b).x + hex(a, b - 1).x
    hex(a, b).y = hex(a, b).y + hex(a, b - 1).y
    hex(a, b).z = hex(a, b).z + hex(a, b - 1).z

  NEXT b
```

Now we have the first hexagram. What we'll do next is rotate this shape four times to construct the others, but while we're here, let's also do the *x*-axis

315

continued from previous page
```
  CLOSE #2
NEXT frame

CLOSE #1
```

Two types of files are generated. There will be 180 BCxxx.INC files that define the positions of the 120 spheres comprising the buckyball, and a BBANIM.BAT file to call the master program, BUCKY.PI. BBANIM writes a file telling BUCKY.PI which geometries to include and what frame number it's on, which controls the sliding image map in the background.

BBANIM.BAT looks like this:

```
echo include "bc000.inc" > bbs.inc
echo define frm  0  >> bbs.inc
\ply\polyray bucky.pi -o bc000.tga
echo include "bc002.inc" > bbs.inc
echo define frm  2  >> bbs.inc
\ply\polyray bucky.pi -o bc002.tga
echo include "bc004.inc" > bbs.inc
echo define frm  4  >> bbs.inc
\ply\polyray bucky.pi - o  bc004.tga
...
```

BBS.INC for frame 0 looks like this:

```
include "bc000.inc"
define frm  0
```

Figure 6-2 Spheres fly out in all directions; pandemonium reigns

And the master program BUCKY.PI looks like this:

```
// BUCKY.PI
// Polyray  file
// Tumbling Buckyball by Jeff Bowermaster

include "\PLY\COLORS.INC"

viewpoint{
   from < 0.0,1.0,-9.0 >
   at   < 0.0,-0.45,0.0 >
   up   < 0.0, 1.0, 0.0 >
   angle 50
   resolution 320,200
   aspect 1.433
}

define bumpy_coral
texture {
   special surface {
      color <1.5,0.75,0>
      normal N + (dnoise(3*W) - white/2)
      ambient 0.2
      diffuse 0.3
      specular white, 0.7
      microfacet Cook 5
      }
   scale <0.05, 0.05, 0.05>
   }

light white*2, <0.0,8.0,-4.0>
include "bbs.inc"

define the_image image("fire.tga")
define flames
   texture {
      special surface {
         color planar_imagemap(the_image, P, 1)
         ambient 0.2
         diffuse 0.8
      }
      rotate <90,0,0>
      scale <20,20,20>
      translate <-0.5, frm/9, -0.5>
   }

object { disc <0,0,10>,<0,0,1>, 20 flames }
```

This is a fairly standard example of external animation using Polyray. A series of complex geometric forms are generated using QuickBasic code, and written to individual include files. A hard-built master file is created that contains the static information, things like the camera location, lighting, and

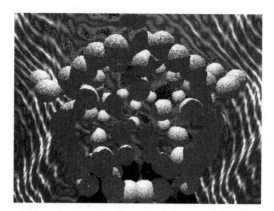

Figure 6-3 Exploding buckyball

textures, as well as variables we may need to change from frame to frame. A line in this master file references a single include file. It contains three things: 1) the name of one of the 180 geometry files the QuickBasic program created, 2) a Frame number, and 3) a line to start Polyray rendering. We get a DOS batch file (BBANIM.BAT) to change the information in this include file for us from frame to frame. This is handled using the redirection operators (> and >>), where screen output is rerouted to a file. A sample image is shown in Figure 6-3.

Comments

It's easy to forget that animations running in batch mode have no frame counter, since in each instance the ray tracer is only rendering a single file. This means that if elements like the chaos background need to be put under the control of the frame counter, we need to include this changing information in the batch file. Also, the names of the image files have to be contained in this file, because we no longer have automatic sequential output.

6.2 How do I...
Tumble a group of interlocking rings?

You'll find the code for this in: PLY\CHAPTER6\RINGS

Problem

Interlocking polygons constitute an interesting set of symmetrical figures. We map the vertices onto the surface of a sphere and move them around so all the points remain on the sphere, and while we can't do it with this code, it's almost possible to generate a set in which all the vertices are spaced equally from one another around a sphere. A whole series of interlocking rings can be created programmatically and tumbled to produce a sloshing, strangely soothing animation.

Technique

Karl Weller made several great examples of interlocking rings. If you stare at them for a few days, you can derive the following QuickBasic code that generates interlocking polygons containing any number of vertices. The ones with three and five vertices seem to look the best, while the ones with an even numbers of vertices generate rings that physically overlap. It's very pleasant to place these figures into an interlocking motion and watch them intertwine.

The following listing (RINGER.BAS) is the simulation code for the interlocking rings. Feel free to change the *sides* variable and see the types of interlocking rings this code creates:

```
DECLARE SUB rotate (a, b, c)
COMMON SHARED xrotate, yrotate, zrotate, rad

' RINGER.BAS - Interlocking Ring Creation Program
' (c) 1993, Jeff Bowermaster, Splat! Graphics

' creates interlocking tumbling polygons
' based on Geometry supplied by Karl Weller in his Ring images

' change the variable sides from 3-9 for various shapes
' three and five seem to work the best, even numbers produce degenerate
' (overlapping) polygons

TYPE Vector
  x AS SINGLE
  y AS SINGLE
  z AS SINGLE
END TYPE

DIM p(10, 9) AS Vector, po(10, 9) AS Vector, pf(10) AS Vector

pi = 3.1415923#
rad = pi / 180

' change this from 3 to 9 for interesting effects
sides = 5

SCREEN 12
WINDOW (-1.6, -1.2)-(1.6, 1.2)

DO WHILE INKEY$ = ""
k = k + 1
```

continued on next page

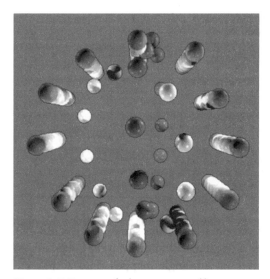

Figure 6-7 Nine rings of spheres prior to tumbling

Technique

What we make here is nine rings, seen edge on in Figure 6-7, each comprised of 16 spheres. We'll assign each sphere its own color, with the amounts of blue and green based on angle around the ring, and red based on which ring it's on. In order to actually see all the colors, we'll make each ring rotate at a different speed. The upper four rings will move clockwise, the lower four rings will move counterclockwise, and the middle ring will slosh back and forth like a washing machine agitator. For a final effect, we'll tumble the twisting structure end over end, and this will bring every sphere into view at some point during the animation.

Steps

The following code (SPHE.BAS) automtically writes the entire Polyray file:

```
' SPHE.BAS
SCREEN 12
WINDOW (-320, -240)-(320, 240)

OPEN "sphe.pi" FOR OUTPUT AS #1

PRINT #1, "//"
PRINT #1, "// SPHERE.PI"
PRINT #1, "//"
PRINT #1, "// Polyray input file - Jeff Bowermaster"
PRINT #1, "// Thanks to Karl Weller for the Colored Space Definition"
```

```
PRINT #1,
PRINT #1, "// define the range of the animation"
PRINT #1,
PRINT #1, "start_frame     0"
PRINT #1, "end_frame      719"
PRINT #1, "total_frames 720"
PRINT #1, "outfile "; CHR$(34); "sphe"; CHR$(34)
PRINT #1,
PRINT #1, "define pi  3.1415927"
PRINT #1, "define rad pi/180"
PRINT #1,
PRINT #1, "// set up the camera"
PRINT #1, "viewpoint {"
PRINT #1, "    from <90,40,400>"
PRINT #1, "    at <0,0,5>"
PRINT #1, "    up <0,1,0>"
PRINT #1, "    angle 45"
PRINT #1, "    resolution 320,200"
PRINT #1, "    aspect 1.433"
PRINT #1, "    }"
PRINT #1,
PRINT #1, "// set up background color & lights"
PRINT #1, "background MidnightBlue *0.5"
PRINT #1, "light  <0.75, 0.75,0.75>,< 0,0,0>"
PRINT #1,

pi = 3.1415927#
rad = pi / 180
r = 140

ring = 1
FOR i = -80 TO 80 STEP 20    ' Nine Rings
   y = SIN(i * rad) * r
   r2 = COS(i * rad) * r
   sphr = 6 * (COS(i * rad) + 1) * (COS(i * rad) + 1)
   ring$ = "ring" + LTRIM$(STR$(ring))
   PRINT #1, USING "define \   \ object {"; ring$
   ring = ring + 1
   FOR j = 0 TO 337.5 STEP 22.5
      x = SIN(j * rad) * r2
      z = COS(j * rad) * r2
      red = ((y / r) + 1!) / 2!
      green = ((x / r2) + 1!) / 2!
      blue = ((z / r2) + 1!) / 2!
      IF j = 0 THEN
          PRINT #1, USING "      object { sphere <####.##, ####.##,####.##>, ⇐
###.## texture { surface { color <#.###, #.###, #.### > ambient 0.4 diffuse ⇐
0.6 reflection 0.95 microfacet Phong 5 }}}"; x, y, z, sphr, red, green, blue
      ELSE
          PRINT #1, USING "    + object { sphere <####.##, ####.##,####.##>, ⇐
###.## texture { surface { color <#.###, #.###, #.### > ambient 0.4 diffuse ⇐
0.6 reflection 0.95 microfacet Phong 5 }}}"; x, y, z, sphr, red, green, blue
      END IF
```

continued on next page

continued from previous page

```
        CIRCLE (x, y), 10
    NEXT j
    PRINT #1, "}"
    PRINT #1,
NEXT i

FOR ring = 1 TO 9
    ring$ = "ring" + LTRIM$(STR$(ring))
    IF ring < 5 THEN
        PRINT #1, USING "object { \    \  rotate <0.0, frame * #.#, 0.0> }"; ⇐
ring$, ring / 2
    ELSE
        IF ring = 5 THEN
            PRINT #1,
            PRINT #1, USING "object { \    \  rotate <0.0, 180*sin(frame *  rad), ⇐
0.0> }"; ring$
            PRINT #1,
        ELSE
            PRINT #1, USING "object { \    \  rotate <0.0, frame * ##.#, 0.0> }"; ⇐
ring$, -(10 - ring) / 2
        END IF
    END IF
NEXT ring
CLOSE #1
```

How It Works

Most of the file SPHERE.PI is color definition and sphere placement. There are nine rings containing 16 spheres each. These rings rotate, with the smaller rings rotating the slowest. The equator ring sloshes back and forth. The entire model flips end over end, and you get to see almost every conceivable color a ray tracer can generate.

```
//
// SPHERE.PI
//
// Polyray input file - Jeff Bowermaster
// Thanks to Karl Weller for the Colored Space Definition

// define the range of the animation

start_frame  0
end_frame    359
total_frames 360
outfile "sphe"

define pi  3.1415927
define rad pi/180
define r   140.0

// set up the camera
viewpoint {
```

```
    from <0,0,-400>
    at <0,0,0>
    up <0,-1,0>
    angle 50
    resolution 320,200
    aspect 1.433
    }

// set up background color & lights
background MidnightBlue*0.75
light   <0.75,0.75,0.75>,<0,0,0>

define ring1 object {
     object { sphere <   0.00, -137.87,  24.31>,   8.26 texture { surface { ⇐
color <0.008, 0.500, 1.000 > ambient 0.4 diffuse 0.6 reflection 0.95 ⇐
microfacet Phong 5 }}}
   + object { sphere <   9.30, -137.87,  22.46>,   8.26 texture { surface { ⇐
color <0.008, 0.691, 0.962 > ambient 0.4 diffuse 0.6 reflection 0.95 ⇐
microfacet Phong 5 }}}
   + object { sphere <  17.19, -137.87,  17.19>,   8.26 texture { surface { ⇐
color <0.008, 0.854, 0.854 > ambient 0.4 diffuse 0.6 reflection 0.95 ⇐
microfacet Phong 5 }}}
   + object { sphere <  22.46, -137.87,   9.30>,   8.26 texture { surface { ⇐
color <0.008, 0.962, 0.691 > ambient 0.4 diffuse 0.6 reflection 0.95 ⇐
microfacet Phong 5 }}}
   + object { sphere <  24.31, -137.87,  -0.00>,   8.26 texture { surface { ⇐
color <0.008, 1.000, 0.500 > ambient 0.4 diffuse 0.6 reflection 0.95 ⇐
microfacet Phong 5 }}}
   + object { sphere <  22.46, -137.87,  -9.30>,   8.26 texture { surface { ⇐
color <0.008, 0.962, 0.309 > ambient 0.4 diffuse 0.6 reflection 0.95 ⇐
microfacet Phong 5 }}}
   + object { sphere <  17.19, -137.87, -17.19>,   8.26 texture { surface { ⇐
color <0.008, 0.854, 0.146 > ambient 0.4 diffuse 0.6 reflection 0.95 ⇐
microfacet Phong 5 }}}
   + object { sphere <   9.30, -137.87, -22.46>,   8.26 texture { surface { ⇐
color <0.008, 0.691, 0.038 > ambient 0.4 diffuse 0.6 reflection 0.95 ⇐
microfacet Phong 5 }}}
   + object { sphere <  -0.00, -137.87, -24.31>,   8.26 texture { surface { ⇐
color <0.008, 0.500, 0.000 > ambient 0.4 diffuse 0.6 reflection 0.95 ⇐
microfacet Phong 5 }}}
   + object { sphere <  -9.30, -137.87, -22.46>,   8.26 texture { surface { ⇐
color <0.008, 0.309, 0.038 > ambient 0.4 diffuse 0.6 reflection 0.95 ⇐
microfacet Phong 5 }}}
   + object { sphere < -17.19, -137.87, -17.19>,   8.26 texture { surface { ⇐
color <0.008, 0.146, 0.146 > ambient 0.4 diffuse 0.6 reflection 0.95 ⇐
microfacet Phong 5 }}}
   + object { sphere < -22.46, -137.87,  -9.30>,   8.26 texture { surface { ⇐
color <0.008, 0.038, 0.309 > ambient 0.4 diffuse 0.6 reflection 0.95 ⇐
microfacet Phong 5 }}}
   + object { sphere < -24.31, -137.87,   0.00>,   8.26 texture { surface { ⇐
color <0.008, 0.000, 0.500 > ambient 0.4 diffuse 0.6 reflection 0.95 ⇐
microfacet Phong 5 }}}
```

continued on next page

Figure 6-11 MTV logo rocks

```
define precessx 5*sin(4*pi*index)
define precessz 5*cos(4*pi*index)
define bob 10 * (sin(2*pi*index)-cos(4*pi*index))

define logo
object {
   M + T + V
   rotate <precessx,0,precessz>
   translate<0,bob,0>
}

logo
```

Figure 6-11 shows the logo bobbing on our yellow sea.

 ## 6.5 How do I...
Cover a sphere evenly with other spheres and make it twinkle?

You'll find the code for this in: PLY\CHAPTER6\TWINKLE

Problem

You'd be surprised how often the need arises for a sphere that's been evenly covered by points. There's surface retriangulation, 3-D morph reference points, and bug eyes, just to mention a few instances. When you need an evenly covered sphere, you usually need it bad.

Technique

Let's go over a few techniques to consider our options. The first method is blind guessing. With RANDOME.BAS, we generate lots of random numbers,

convert these to polar coordinates that map onto a sphere, then test each
new point to see if it's too close to one that's already there. If it is, we chuck
it. If it's not, we keep it and move on. It works, but it's slow and the surface
coverage is not very even:

```
'RANDOME.BAS
DECLARE SUB rotate (d, e, f)

TYPE vector
    x AS SINGLE
    y AS SINGLE
    z AS SINGLE
END TYPE

DIM red(16), green(16), blue(16), v(5000) AS vector
COMMON SHARED rad, xrotate, yrotate
SCREEN 12

FOR y = 1 TO 4
    FOR x = 1 TO 4
        colornum = x + ((y - 1) * 4) - 1
        READ red(colornum), green(colornum), blue(colornum)
        col = 65536 * blue(colornum) + 256 * green(colornum) + red(colornum)
        PALETTE colornum, col
        COLOR colornum
    NEXT x
NEXT y


'rainbow palette

DATA  0,  0,  0
DATA 32,  0,  0
DATA 42,  0,  0
DATA 58, 16,  0
DATA 63, 32,  0
DATA 58, 56,  0
DATA 16, 42,  0
DATA  0, 30, 36
DATA  0, 20, 40
DATA  0, 10, 48
DATA  0,  0, 63
DATA 20,  0, 53
DATA 23,  0, 29
DATA 19,  7, 17
DATA 50, 40, 45
DATA 63, 63, 63

pi = 3.13159
rad = pi / 180
min = .05
min2 = min * min
diam = min / 2
```

continued on next page

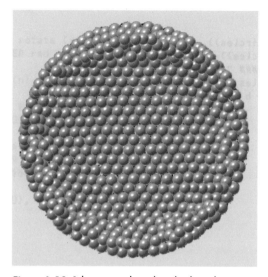

Figure 6-13 Sphere covered evenly with other spheres

```
OPEN "dome" FOR INPUT AS #1
OPEN "d:\ply\dat\hex\dome.pi" FOR OUTPUT AS #2
FOR x = 1 TO 642
   INPUT #1, a, b, c
   PRINT #2, USING "object { sphere <##.######, ##.######, ##.######>, 0.1 ⇐
matte__white }"; a, b, c
NEXT x
CLOSE #1
CLOSE #2
```

This array of spheres is enclosed inside a larger sphere, and spotlights are placed around it in the following listing (DOME.PI). A combination of blue and coral lights above gives it a Maxfield Parrish feel. We rotate the mass and shrink the sizes of each sphere until they only catch the rays occasionally. With the darkness below and lighting from above, the sparkling is striking:

```
// DOME.PI - Semi Sorta Geodesic Dome Type Deal

start_frame 0
end_frame 179
total_frames 180

outfile "dome"

include "\PLY\COLORS.INC"

viewpoint {
   from <-3,0,-3>      //-5,0,-3
   at <0,0,3>
```

```
   up <0,0,1>
   angle 70
   resolution 480,480   // 160,480
   aspect 1             // 0.33
   }

spot_light < 2, 1, 0>,<-5,-5, 5>,<0,0,0>,3,15,30
spot_light < 0.5, 0, 1>,< 5,-5, 5>,<0,0,0>,3,15,30
spot_light < 0, 0, 0.5>,< 5, 5, 5>,<0,0,0>,3,15,30
spot_light < 0.25, 0, 1>,<-5, 5, 5>,<0,0,0>,3,15,30

spot_light < 0.25, 0.5, 1>,<0, 0, -5>,<0,0,0>,3,5,20

define bright texture { matte { color white*2} }
object { sphere <0.0,0.0,0.5>, 9 bright }

define pi 3.14159
define rad pi/180

// shrink and rotate
define radius 0.1*(1.1+cos(rad*frame*2))/2

object {
   object { sphere < 0.101056,  0.000000,  0.994881>, radius matte_white }
 + object { sphere < 0.050528,  0.087517,  0.994881>, radius matte_white }
 + object { sphere <-0.050528,  0.087517,  0.994881>, radius matte_white }
 + object { sphere <-0.101056,  0.000000,  0.994881>, radius matte_white }
 + object { sphere <-0.050528, -0.087517,  0.994881>, radius matte_white }
 + object { sphere < 0.050528, -0.087517,  0.994881>, radius matte_white }
 + object { sphere < 0.150384,  0.086824,  0.984808>, radius matte_white }
 + object { sphere < 0.000000,  0.173648,  0.984808>, radius matte_white }
 + object { sphere <-0.150383,  0.086824,  0.984808>, radius matte_white }
 + object { sphere <-0.150384, -0.086824,  0.984808>, radius matte_white }
 + object { sphere <-0.000001, -0.173648,  0.984808>, radius matte_white }
 + object { sphere < 0.150383, -0.086825,  0.984808>, radius matte_white }
 + object { sphere < 0.201078,  0.000000,  0.979575>, radius matte_white }
 + object { sphere < 0.100539,  0.174139,  0.979575>, radius matte_white }
...
(600 sphere)
...
 + object { sphere <-0.325566,  0.945518, -0.001730>, radius matte_white }
 + object { sphere <-0.981625,  0.190811, -0.001730>, radius matte_white }
 + object { sphere <-0.656060, -0.754706, -0.001730>, radius matte_white }
 + object { sphere < 0.325564, -0.945518, -0.001730>, radius matte_white }
 + object { sphere < 0.981625, -0.190813, -0.001730>, radius matte_white }
   rotate <0,0,frame*2>
}
```

How It Works

We're inside a large sphere and below this dome. There are four very brightly colored spotlights shining on our dome, using Maxfield Parrish colors for mood:

```
spot_light < 2, 1, 0>,<-5,-5, 5>,<0,0,0>,3,15,30
spot_light < 0.5, 0, 1>,< 5,-5, 5>,<0,0,0>,3,15,30
spot_light < 0, 0, 0.5>,< 5, 5, 5>,<0,0,0>,3,15,30
spot_light < 0.25, 0, 1>,<-5, 5, 5>,<0,0,0>,3,15,30
```

One spotlight is directly below the sphere dome, shining up:

```
spot_light < 0.25, 0.5, 1>,<0, 0, -5>,<0,0,0>,3,5,20
```

The last line in the sphere dome definition makes the whole thing rotate.

The beauty of this animation is that, other than the rotation, it really only has one other moving part. The frame-dependent expression

```
// shrink and rotate
define radius 0.1*(1.1+cos(rad*frame*2))/2
```

sets the radius for all the spheres in the dome to vary between 0.05 and 1.15. Without antialiasing, 0.05 is so small that the ray tracer will only randomly register that they're there, which makes them twinkle (see Figure 6-14).

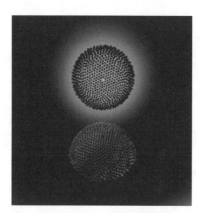

Figure 6-14 Twinkle twinkle little sphere

CHAPTER
7

7

BLOBS

Blobs are an affectionate name given to objects that, for lack of a better description look like, well... blobs. They are built out of any number of smaller units called metaballs, each of which is defined by a location, a radius, and a strength. Each metaball generates a field that defines a value for every point in the space surrounding it. The size of this field is set by its radius; the magnitude of this field is set by its strength. When it comes time to render a surface, the field strength contributions for all the metaballs at any particular point in 3D space are added together, and wherever this value equals the threshold value, a surface element appears. Some examples are shown in Figure 7-1.

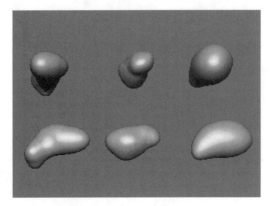

Figure 7-1 Blobs

There are presently two valid methods for specifying blobs in Polyray. The "new" way goes like this:

blob threshold:
    sphere <x, y, z>, strength, radius,
    cylinder <x0, y0, z0>, <x1, y1, z1>, strength, radius,
    plane <nx, ny, nz>, d, strength, dist,
    ...

Here the threshold defines where the surface forms, and the strength and radius specify the potential field surrounding each controlling element.
The "old" way, back in the days when the only type of blob was spherical, went like this:

blob threshold:
    strength, radius,<x, y, z>,
    strength, radius,<x, y, z>,
    strength, radius,<x, y, z>,
    ...

The parser in Polyray (which translates text files you write into meaningful syntax Polyray uses to create the actual images) can deal with both formats, but if you use the new format, you'll have both planar and cylindrical blobs to play with.

The best way to learn about blobs is to play with them. A most remarkable example of what blobs are capable of is contained in the sample files that come with Polyray called SQUISH (see Figure 7-1). This animation uses 16 metaballs, each moving independent of the others. Some orbit, while some slide back and forth. The squirming animation that develops resembles a clump of water in free fall.

Blobs are capable of generating some remarkably lifelike forms, but they do have limitations. They aren't quite as simple to use as modeling clay. You'll have to select the proper strength, radius, and threshold values or else it will end up looking like you're just sticking a lot of spheres together. Also, the more metaballs your blobs have, the longer the rendering times will be.

7.1 How do I...
Visualize potential fields about objects?

You'll find the code for this in: PLY\CHAPTER7\3LEVELS

Problem

Volume rendering is an exciting visualization field. It allows you to see the internal structure of solid objects, as semi-transparent layers or cut-away views. It can be used to illustrate the internal structures of complex objects such as hips and skulls. People interested in such things are usually either recovering from exposure to sudden changes in their inertial reference frames (Editor's note: we think he means "car crashes") or gainfully employed in assisting them. We won't deal with such lofty topics here, since the data sets are enormous and the equipment used to gather them very expensive. With enough data storage capacity and processing power, we could use the following principles to render 3-D volumes. We'll use blobs of various thresholds to simulate our volume data, and move them around to give a good 3-D feel to them.

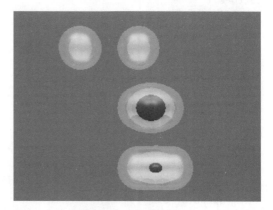

Figure 7-2 Oscillating three-level blob

363

Technique

Potential fields, like an electric field around an object, can be made visible by rendering surfaces of constant electric potential. Additional 3D information can be imparted by using independent, multilayered, transparent blobs. While metaballs of one blob add together to determine the final shape, separate blobs do not influence each other. The following simple program (3LEVEL1.PI) is a three-layered blob, with one of its metaballs fixed and the other one oscillating back and forth along the x axis (Figure 7-2).

```
// 3LEVEL1.PI

start_frame 0
end_frame 30
total_frames 30

outfile 3lev

include "\PLY\COLORS.INC"

viewpoint {
   from <0,0,-8>
   at <0,0,0>
   up <0,1,0>
   angle 30
   resolution 200,100
   aspect 2*1.43/1.6
   }

background SkyBlue
light 0.6 * white, <-15,30,-25>
light 0.6 * white, < 15,30,-25>


define yellow_glass
texture {
   surface {
      ambient yellow, 0.05
      diffuse yellow, 0.05
      specular 0.6
      reflection white, 0.1
      transmission white, 0.95, 1.0
      }
   }

define green_glass
texture {
   surface {
      ambient green, 0.05
      diffuse green, 0.05
      specular 0.2
```

```
         reflection white, 0.1
         transmission white, 0.95, 1.0
         }
    }

define blue_glass
texture {
    surface {
        ambient blue, 0.2
        diffuse blue, 0.6
        specular 0.6
        reflection blue, 0.1
        }
    }

define pi 3.14159
define index frame/total_frames

define a 3*sin(2*pi*index)

object {
    blob 0.5:
        1.0, 2.0, <0, 0, 0>,
        1.0, 2.0, <a, 0, 0>
    yellow_glass
}


object {
    blob 0.75:
        0.9, 2.0, <0, 0, 0>,
        0.9, 2.0, <a, 0, 0>
    green_glass
}

object {
    blob 1.0:
        0.8, 2.0, <0, 0, 0>,
        0.8, 2.0, <a, 0, 0>
    blue_glass
}
```

How It Works

We move one blob element back and forth three units, and give all the blob elements the same radius, but vary the strengths from 1.0 for the outer yellow blob to 0.8 for the inner blue blob. The interior blue glass ball disappears, because it doesn't have enough strength to remain solid once the metaballs defining it move more than about one unit apart. The two outer layers remain visible after they separate because they form at lower thresholds.

continued from previous page

```
define radius 1.5
object {
   blob threshold:
      sphere <a, b, 0>, strength, radius,
      sphere <a,-b, 0>, strength, radius,
      sphere <-a, b, 0>, strength, radius,
      sphere <-a,-b, 0>, strength, radius,
   yellow_glass
}

define radius 1.0
object {
   blob threshold:
      sphere <a, b, 0>, strength, radius,
      sphere <a,-b, 0>, strength, radius,
      sphere <-a, b, 0>, strength, radius,
      sphere <-a,-b, 0>, strength, radius,
   green_glass
}

define radius 0.5
object {
   blob threshold:
      sphere <a, b, 0>, strength, radius,
      sphere <a,-b, 0>, strength, radius,
      sphere <-a, b, 0>, strength, radius,
      sphere <-a,-b, 0>, strength, radius,
   blue_glass
}
```

3LEVEL2.PI generates this dividing/kneading motion for our four blobs by using four conditional statements that define their motions. The animation is divided into four parts. During the first quarter, we smoothly split the blob

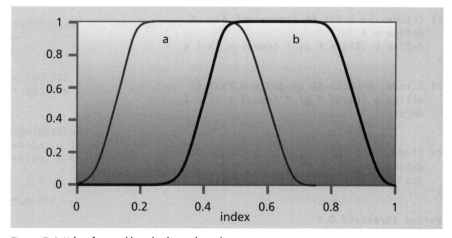

Figure 7-4 Values for a and b set by the conditional statements

into two parts using a cosine spline, by assigning one blob positive values for *a*, the other one negative values. We split it into four parts during the second quarter, this time using positive and negative values for *b*. We rejoin the first split during the third quarter, and then collapse the figure back into a single object during the fourth quarter. The values determined by the conditional code are shown in Figure 7-4.

```
if (index >= 0 && index < 0.25) {
   define a (1 - COS(4 * pi * index)) / 2
   define b 0
}

if ((index >= 0.25) && (index < 0.5)) {
   define a 1
   define b (COS(4 * pi * index) + 1) / 2
}

if ((index >= 0.5) && (index < 0.75)) {
   define a (COS(4 * pi * index) + 1) / 2
   define b 1
}

if (index >= 0.75) {
   define a 0
   define b (1 - COS(4 * pi * index)) / 2
}
```

Now we've done a 1-D and a 2-D blob splitting animation. Let's bump it up to 3-D. We'll place it over some textured surface and rotate the viewpoint for some better depth clues. 3LEVEL3.PI is shown here:

```
// 3LEVEL3.PI
start_frame 0
end_frame 179
total_frames 180

define index frame/total_frames

outfile 3lev

include "\PLY\COLORS.INC"

viewpoint {
   from rotate(<5,5,-5>,<0,-360*index,0>)
   at <0,0,0>
   up <0,1,0>
   angle 30
   resolution 200,200
   aspect 1*1.433/1.6
   }

background MidnightBlue
```

continued on next page

CHAPTER SEVEN

continued from previous page

```
light 0.6 * white, <-15,30,-25>
light 0.6 * white, < 15,30,-25>


define yellow_glass
texture {
   surface {
      ambient yellow, 0.05
      diffuse yellow, 0.05
      specular 0.6
      reflection white, 0.1
      transmission white, 0.95, 1.0
      }
   }

define green_glass
texture {
   surface {
      ambient green, 0.05
      diffuse green, 0.05
      specular 0.2
      reflection white, 0.1
      transmission white, 0.95, 1.0
      }
   }

define blue_glass
texture {
   surface {
      ambient blue, 0.2
      diffuse blue, 0.6
      specular 0.6
      reflection blue, 0.1
      }
   }

define pi 3.14159
define index frame/total_frames

define a 0.7071+sin(2*pi*index)
define b 0.7071+sin(2*pi*(index+0.33))
define c 0.7071+sin(2*pi*(index+0.66))


define threshold 0.9
define strength 1.0

define radius 1.5
object {
   blob threshold:
      sphere <a, b, c>, strength, radius,
      sphere <a,-b, c>, strength, radius,
      sphere <-a, b, c>, strength, radius,
      sphere <-a,-b, c>, strength, radius,
```

```
        sphere <a, b, -c>, strength, radius,
        sphere <a,-b, -c>, strength, radius,
        sphere <-a, b,-c>, strength, radius,
        sphere <-a,-b,-c>, strength, radius
    yellow_glass
}

define radius 1.0
object {
    blob threshold:
        sphere <a, b, c>, strength, radius,
        sphere <a,-b, c>, strength, radius,
        sphere <-a, b, c>, strength, radius,
        sphere <-a,-b, c>, strength, radius,
        sphere <a, b,-c>, strength, radius,
        sphere <a,-b,-c>, strength, radius,
        sphere <-a, b,-c>, strength, radius,
        sphere <-a,-b,-c>, strength, radius
    green_glass
}

define radius 0.5
object {
    blob threshold:
        sphere <a, b, c>, strength, radius,
        sphere <a,-b, c>, strength, radius,
        sphere <-a, b, c>, strength, radius,
        sphere <-a,-b, c>, strength, radius,
        sphere <a, b,-c>, strength, radius,
        sphere <a,-b,-c>, strength, radius,
        sphere <-a, b,-c>, strength, radius,
        sphere <-a,-b,-c>, strength, radius
    blue_glass
}


// yellow dented/wrinkled appearance
define dented_plutonium
texture {
    noise surface {
        color <1.0, 0.5, 0.1>*1.1
        normal 1
        frequency 2
        bump_scale 3
        ambient 0.2
        diffuse 0.5
        specular 0.7
        microfacet Reitz 10
        }
    scale <0.2, 0.2, 0.2>
    }

object {disc <0,-2.5,0>,<0,1,0>,10 dented_plutonium }
```

continued from previous page

```
PRINT #1, "    from <3,3,-3>"
PRINT #1, "    at <0,0,0>"
PRINT #1, "    up <0,1,0>"
PRINT #1, "    angle 45"
PRINT #1, "    resolution 320,200"
PRINT #1, "    aspect 1.43"
PRINT #1, "    }"
PRINT #1,
PRINT #1, "// set up background color & lights"
PRINT #1, "background skyblue"
PRINT #1, "light <10,0,-10>"
PRINT #1, "light <-10,0,-10>"
PRINT #1,
PRINT #1, "include "; CHR$(34); "\PLY\COLORS.INC"; CHR$(34)
PRINT #1,
PRINT #1, "define pi 3.14159"
PRINT #1, "define rad pi/180"
PRINT #1,
PRINT #1, "define threshold 0.002 + 0.01 * (cos(rad*4*frame)+1)"
PRINT #1, "define strength  0.01"
PRINT #1, "define range 0.4"
PRINT #1,
PRINT #1, "// fire 1"
PRINT #1,

FOR b = 1 TO 16

    PRINT #1, "object {"
    PRINT #1, "    blob threshold:"

stp = 1
maxa = 360
FOR angle = 1 TO maxa STEP stp

    FOR a = 1 TO 16

        xrotate = COS(rad * angle)
        yrotate = SIN(rad * angle)
        zrotate = 1

'rotate

        CALL rotate(cube(a).x, cube(a).y, cube(a).z)

    NEXT a

'generate the metaballs
    IF angle MOD 10 = 0 THEN
        IF angle < maxa THEN
            PRINT #1, USING "strength, range, < ##.#####, ##.#####, ##.##### >,"; ⇐
cube(b).x * angle / 360, cube(b).y * angle / 360, cube(b).z * angle / 360
        ELSE
```

```
        PRINT #1, USING "strength, range, < ##.#####, ##.#####, ##.##### >"; ⇐
cube(b).x * angle / 360, cube(b).y * angle / 360, cube(b).z * angle / 360
      END IF
      CIRCLE (cube(b).x * angle / 360, cube(b).y * angle / 360), angle / ⇐
1800, INT(2 * (cube(b).z + 3))
      last(b) = cube(b)
   END IF
NEXT angle

   PRINT #1, "   root_solver Ferrari"
   PRINT #1, "   u_steps 20"
   PRINT #1, "   v_steps 20"
   READ texture$
   PRINT #1, "   "; texture$
   PRINT #1, "   rotate <0, 4*frame, 0>"

   PRINT #1, "   }"

PRINT #1,
NEXT b
CLOSE #1

DATA reflective_grey
DATA reflective_blue
DATA reflective_red
DATA reflective_green
DATA reflective_orange
DATA reflective_yellow
DATA reflective_cyan
DATA reflective_brown
DATA reflective_tan
DATA reflective_coral
DATA reflective_gold
DATA shiny_red
DATA reflective_blue
DATA shiny_blue
DATA shiny_orange
DATA shiny_yellow

SUB rotate (x, y, z)

    x0 = x
    y0 = y
    z0 = z

    x1 = x0
    y1 = y0 * COS(xrotate * rad) - z0 * SIN(xrotate * rad)
    z1 = y0 * SIN(xrotate * rad) + z0 * COS(xrotate * rad)

    x2 = z1 * SIN(yrotate * rad) + x1 * COS(yrotate * rad)
    y2 = y1
    z2 = z1 * COS(yrotate * rad) - x1 * SIN(yrotate * rad)
```

continued on next page

continued from previous page

```
    x3 = x2 * COS(zrotate * rad) - y2 * SIN(zrotate * rad)
    y3 = x2 * SIN(zrotate * rad) + y2 * COS(zrotate * rad)
    z3 = z2

    x = x3
    y = y3
    z = z3

END SUB
```

This generates the following Polyray data file:

```
//  BANA.PI
//  Bananarama - Spiral Blob Mass
//
// Polyray input file - Jeff Bowermaster

// define the range of the animation
start_frame   0
end_frame     89
total_frames 90
outfile bana

// set up the camera
viewpoint {
   from <3,3,-3>
   at <0,0,0>
   up <0,1,0>
   angle 45
   resolution 320,200
   aspect 1.43
   }

// set up background color & lights
background skyblue
light <10,0,-10>
light <-10,0,-10>

include "\ply\colors.inc"

define pi 3.14159
define rad pi/180

define threshold 0.002 + 0.01 * (cos(rad*4*frame)+1)
define strength  0.01
define range 0.4

//  fire 1

object {
   blob threshold:
strength, range, <  0.02354,   0.02703,   0.03209 >,
strength, range, <  0.04122,   0.05037,   0.07087 >,
```

```
strength, range, <  0.05771,   0.06867,   0.11308 >,
strength, range, <  0.07750,   0.08327,   0.15523 >,
strength, range, <  0.10378,   0.09792,   0.19368 >,
strength, range, <  0.13732,   0.11786,   0.22491 >,
strength, range, <  0.17601,   0.14867,   0.24564 >,
strength, range, <  0.21480,   0.19489,   0.25304 >,
strength, range, <  0.24625,   0.25866,   0.24485 >,
strength, range, <  0.26172,   0.33879,   0.21955 >,
strength, range, <  0.25278,   0.43020,   0.17643 >,
strength, range, <  0.21288,   0.52406,   0.11565 >,
strength, range, <  0.13890,   0.60864,   0.03831 >,
strength, range, <  0.03230,   0.67066,  -0.05362 >,
strength, range, < -0.10031,   0.69716,  -0.15730 >,
strength, range, < -0.24734,   0.67748,  -0.26915 >,
strength, range, < -0.39322,   0.60513,  -0.38494 >,
strength, range, < -0.51997,   0.47924,  -0.49996 >,
strength, range, < -0.60933,   0.30532,  -0.60922 >,
strength, range, < -0.64512,   0.09522,  -0.70759 >,
strength, range, < -0.61541,  -0.13375,  -0.79007 >,
strength, range, < -0.51440,  -0.36045,  -0.85196 >,
strength, range, < -0.34356,  -0.56217,  -0.88908 >,
strength, range, < -0.11197,  -0.71726,  -0.89796 >,
strength, range, <  0.16427,  -0.80769,  -0.87602 >,
strength, range, <  0.46355,  -0.82143,  -0.82171 >,
strength, range, <  0.76100,  -0.75413,  -0.73463 >,
strength, range, <  1.03139,  -0.61000,  -0.61560 >,
strength, range, <  1.25206,  -0.40159,  -0.46672 >,
strength, range, <  1.40585,  -0.14852,  -0.29132 >,
strength, range, <  1.48329,   0.12485,  -0.09390 >,
strength, range, <  1.48393,   0.39236,   0.11995 >,
strength, range, <  1.41651,   0.62945,   0.34371 >,
strength, range, <  1.29783,   0.81640,   0.57015 >,
strength, range, <  1.15053,   0.94095,   0.79155 >,
strength, range, <  1.00000,   1.00005,   0.99995 >
    root_solver Ferrari
    u_steps 20
    v_steps 20
    reflective_grey
    rotate <0, 4*frame, 0>
    }

...
(repeats for a total of 16 bananas)
```

The resulting image has some really odd motion, and is shown in Figure 7-8.

How It Works

We get QuickBasic to manufacture some oddly shaped intertwining spirals, assign some colorful textures to them, and vary the threshold where the surfaces form to make them inflate and deflate as they rotate.

CHAPTER SEVEN

continued from previous page

```
light <10,-10,-10>
light <-10,-10,-10>

define b1 <    0.000,    1.000,    0.000 >
define b2 <    1.000,    0.000,    0.000 >
define b3 <    0.000,    0.000,    0.000 >
define b4 <   -1.000,    0.000,    0.000 >
define b5 <    0.000,   -1.000,    0.000 >

define r1 0.96
define r2 0.96
define r3 0.98
define r4 0.99
define r5 1.00
define r6 1.01
define r7 1.02
define r8 1.03
define r9 1.04
define range 0.25

if (frame < total_frames/2)
   define strength range*10^(frame/total_frames)+0.7
else
    define strength range*10^((total_frames_frame)/total_frames)+0.7

define xrot frame*360/total.frames
define threshold \

//   fire 4

object {
   blob   threshold:
       strength, r1,b1,
       strength, r1,b2,
       strength, r1,b3,
       strength, r1,b4,
       strength, r1,b5
   root_solver Ferrari
   u_steps 20
   v_steps 20
   reflective_coral
   rotate <xrot,xrot, 0>
   translate <-2.500,-1.000, 1.500 >
   }

object {
   blob   threshold:
       strength, r2,b1,
       strength, r2,b2,
       strength, r2,b3,
       strength, r2,b4,
       strength, r2,b5
   root_solver Ferrari
```

```
         u_steps 20
         v_steps 20
         reflective_coral
         rotate <xrot,0, 0>
         translate < 0.000,-1.000, 1.500 >
         }

object {
      blob   threshold:
         strength, r3,b1,
         strength, r3,b2,
         strength, r3,b3,
         strength, r3,b4,
         strength, r3,b5
      root_solver Ferrari
      u_steps 20
      v_steps 20
      reflective_coral
      rotate <xrot,-xrot, 0>
      translate < 2.500,-1.000, 1.500 >
      }
object {
      blob   threshold:
         strength, r4,b1,
         strength, r4,b2,
         strength, r4,b3,
         strength, r4,b4,
         strength, r4,b5
      root_solver Ferrari
      u_steps 20
      v_steps 20
      reflective_coral
      rotate <-xrot,xrot, 0>
      translate <-2.500, 0.000,-0.250 >
      }
object {
      blob   threshold:
         strength, r5,b1,
         strength, r5,b2,
         strength, r5,b3,
         strength, r5,b4,
         strength, r5,b5
      root_solver Ferrari
      u_steps 20
      v_steps 20
      reflective_coral
      rotate <-xrot,0, 0>
      translate < 0.000, 0.000,-0.250 >
      }

object {
      blob   threshold:
```

continued on next page

continued from previous page

```
        strength, r6,b1,
        strength, r6,b2,
        strength, r6,b3,
        strength, r6,b4,
        strength, r6,b5
   root_solver Ferrari
   u_steps 20
   v_steps 20
   reflective_coral
   rotate <-xrot,-xrot, 0>
   translate < 2.500, 0.000,-0.250 >
   }
object {
   blob  threshold:
        strength, r7,b1,
        strength, r7,b2,
        strength, r7,b3,
        strength, r7,b4,
        strength, r7,b5
   root_solver Ferrari
   u_steps 20
   v_steps 20
   reflective_coral
   rotate <xrot,xrot, 0>
   translate <-2.500, 1.000,-2.000 >
   }
object {
   blob  threshold:
        strength, r8,b1,
        strength, r8,b2,
        strength, r8,b3,
        strength, r8,b4,
        strength, r8,b5
   root_solver Ferrari
   u_steps 20
   v_steps 20
   reflective_coral
   rotate <xrot,0, 0>
   translate < 0.000, 1.000,-2.000 >
   }
object {
   blob  threshold:
        strength, r9,b1,
        strength, r9,b2,
        strength, r9,b3,
        strength, r9,b4,
        strength, r9,b5
   root_solver Ferrari
   u_steps 20
   v_steps 20
   reflective_coral
   rotate <xrot,-xrot, 0>
   translate < 2.500, 1.000,-2.000 >
   }
```

How It Works

This is an example of an animation created to test out the control variables for what was a new graphics primitive at the time this code was written. The objects' reflections surface rotate making this interesting animation stand out (Figure 7-10). This also serves as an example of how to explore aspects of ray tracing code when you're interested in seeing how parameters affect the formations of surfaces.

We select nine values for the radii of the blob elements:

```
define r1 0.96
define r2 0.96
define r3 0.98
define r4 0.99
define r5 1.00
define r6 1.01
define r7 1.02
define r8 1.03
define r9 1.04
```

then vary the strength parameter during the animation and watch the results:

```
if (frame < total_frames/2)
    define strength 0.00075*10^(frame/80)
else
    define strength 0.00075*10^((total_frames-frame)/80)
```

Granted, this is over a fairly narrow range, and it resulted from explorations with wider ranges when the old Polyray bug was active.

Comments

This type of exploration is particularly useful when hunting for new textures, since you can cover a lot of ground automatically, programming your animations to search out and explore what the various parameters control.

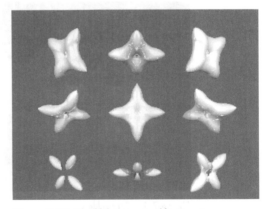

Figure 7-10 Nine blob crosses tumbling in unison

Figure 7-12 Midpoint view inside our tunnel

How It Works

This is a simple but beautiful animation. A single blob tunnel is intersected by a series of other tunnels at right angles. The camera viewpoint moves down the tunnel, accompanied by a light. The phase of the surface normals for the rippling texture changes as we move down the tube. We proceed from one end of the tunnel to the other. A midpoint view is shown in Figure 7-12.

Comments

The addition of other elements drifting past inside the tunnel would enhance the sense of motion. However, this animation took over a week to render as it stands. The variable "reflection" in the *blue_ripple* texture definition can be commented out to speed up the rendering with only a minor impact on the image.

7.6 How do I...
Fly through tunnels on an asteroid?

You'll find the code for this in: PLY\CHAPTER7\ASTEROID

Problem

One of the real challenges of computer animation is the coordination of a flight path inside an object at close quarters. One example of this is a fight through the interior of a blob. As was mentioned in Section 3.9, it was quite a revelation to discover that not only are blobs hollow, they contain tunnels, arches, caverns, and other interesting interior structures. A simple arrangement of metaballs in a regular cubical structure generates an amazing three-level blob cavern. It's a real challenge to design a spline path that threads these caverns without smashing through the walls.

The other chief difficulty in flying around randomly inside an object is the dreaded "up" vector. The definition of the camera's viewpoint is fine every place except where the camera is pointing either directly up or directly down. At these two points, the idea of "up" becomes undefined, so the camera no longer maintains a stable orientation. It can flip suddenly upside down with the slightest motion on either side of where "up" is, resulting in your scene doing an abrupt 180° turn. The asteroid flythrough could deal with this problem by continuously redefining the position of up so that it always points to the center of the asteroid, but this numbs the sense of up and down (well, actually, it kills it entirely). Instead, we first run a small test animation, determine at what frame numbers the flips occurs, and then correct the camera orientation to obtain consistent camera viewpoint.

Technique

The most demanding part of this animation was threading the flight path through the tunnels. A cutaway view reveals where the bottoms of the tunnels are, and given the regular placement of metaballs, leads to a collection of spline control points that steer us through the caverns and lets us exit without a scratch.

The first step was to render the asteroid we created with the outer layers removed to give us an idea where the floors of the tunnels were. Once you realize that the metaballs are placed on the corners and along the edges of a cube, it's not surprising to find that the tunnel also lines up with these features. A collection of data points based on the edges and corners of the cube line up with the insides of the tunnels. It then becomes a matter of threading these points in the proper sequence with a spline line to smoothly go from one clear area to the next, eventually moving down each tunnel. The initial guess is shown in Table 7-1:

X	Y	Z
0	0	2
0	0	1
1	1	1
0	1	0

continued on next page

CHAPTER SEVEN

continued from previous page

```
    }


define s 8

define collection
object {
    asteroid {translate <-s,-s,-s>}
  + asteroid {translate <-s,-s, 0>}
  + asteroid {translate <-s,-s, s>}

  + asteroid {translate <-s, 0,-s>}
  + asteroid {translate <-s, 0, 0>}
  + asteroid {translate <-s, 0, s>}

  + asteroid {translate <-s, s,-s>}
  + asteroid {translate <-s, s, 0>}
  + asteroid {translate <-s, s, s>}


  + asteroid {translate < 0,-s,-s>}
  + asteroid {translate < 0,-s, 0>}
  + asteroid {translate < 0,-s, s>}

  + asteroid {translate < 0, 0,-s>}
  + asteroid {translate < 0, 0, 0>}
  + asteroid {translate < 0, 0, s>}

  + asteroid {translate < 0, s,-s>}
  + asteroid {translate < 0, s, 0>}
  + asteroid {translate < 0, s, s>}


  + asteroid {translate < s,-s,-s>}
  + asteroid {translate < s,-s, 0>}
  + asteroid {translate < s,-s, s>}

  + asteroid {translate < s, 0,-s>}
  + asteroid {translate < s, 0, 0>}
  + asteroid {translate < s, 0, s>}

  + asteroid {translate < s, s,-s>}
  + asteroid {translate < s, s, 0>}
  + asteroid {translate < s, s, s>}
}


// main one
asteroid
if(inc==1) {collection {translate <0, 0, -2*s> }}
if(inc==2) {collection {translate < 2*s, 0, 0> }}
```

Rather than making a single pass through this asteroid, a loop point was made by flying in through one side and exiting out the other, and by having a field of 27 other asteroids called *collection* appear at the beginning and the end of the flight, controlled by the variable *inc*. This makes it appear that you're in an asteroid field, but once you are inside the caverns there's little point in having 27 extra blobs slow down the rendering. Both *collection*s are made to line up exactly, so that the first frame aligns with the last. This makes it appear as if you were entering the same asteroid over and over. To maintain similar lighting at both ends, all light sources track the motion of the camera and end up exactly where they were when they began, with respect to the asteroid we're about to enter. There's still a flash as some of the light sources emerge from behind some blobs, but it's minor.

The asteroids in the array are all separated by eight units. Once you're outside the asteroid, you accelerate away from one towards the next one. Conditional code generates frames that start at the midpoint between two blob asteroids and end at roughly the same position.

Views of the asteroid field and the inside of the tunnel are shown in Figures 7-14 and 7-15.

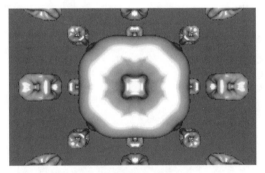

Figure 7-14 The asteroid field

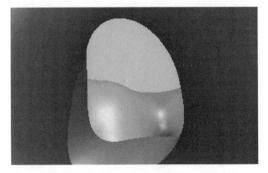

Figure 7-15 Inside a tunnel in the asteroid

CHAPTER

8

8

RECURSION

Many patterns in nature derive their pleasant symmetry as well as their low level details to some very simple construction rules applied across a wide range of scales in an image. For example, an object is defined as an assemblage of smaller objects using some rule. Those objects are themselves defined using this same rule, and the process continues down the resolution scale until the details become too small to see or the computer gags on the number of objects it's asked to generate. Calling image definition code from within a layer that uses that same code is known as recursion, and it automates the process of defining finely detailed objects.

Figure 8-1 A recursive tree

Take a look at the L-system fractal tree in Figure 8-1. The entire tree was defined with just two parameters: the angle of the branches and the rate at which the branches get smaller. The computer just iterates the code to get the complex shape of the tree.

To create such recursive images with Polyray, we can either use external files and batch animation, or use nested defines in the ray tracer, such as:

```
define layer1
object {
   object { sphere ... }
 + object { cylinder... }
 + ...
}

define layer2
object {
   object {layer1 scale <...> translate <...> }
 + object {layer1 scale <...> translate <...> }
 + ...
}

define layer3
object {
   object {layer2 scale <...> translate <...> }
 + object {layer2 scale <...> translate <...> }
 + ...
}

...
```

We'll play with two kinds of recursion: physical recursion that generate complex objects from simple definitions, and motion recursion, where the movements of smaller pieces of an object are synchronized with the movements of larger pieces. Physical recursion results in an object being self-similar; in other words, parts of it resemble other parts, only on different scales. Motion recursion may involve something like taking the seed element for a recursive object and rotating it, setting all the smaller pieces into coordinated motions that mimic the larger motion. This is very easy in Polyray, since motion can be included as part of an object when it's defined, and the effects can be bizarre.

More so than any other chapter, this one is extremely open-ended. The examples just provide the starting point for limitless exploration into recursion and self-similar animations.

8.1 How do I...
Grow an L-system fan?

You'll find the code for this in: PLY\CHAPTER8\FAN

Problem

Figure 8-1 shows a detailed object that was generated not by the tedious process of hand crafting each little item, but by giving instructions to a computer that takes simple specifications and does the work for us. We'll use recursion to generate a branched fractal tree, and animate the variables to illustrate their effects.

Technique

A recursive program is written in QuickBasic, modeled on code found in an excellent book by Roger Stevens, *Fractal Programming in C* (M&T Books 1989). It has three parts. A main routine defines control variables and draws a seed element. A recursive subroutine is used to draw the branches. At each new branch, we need to know what the angle was from the last branch, and build the next one with respect to it. New branches form to the left and right of the previous ones. The main difference between recursion in QuickBasic and recursion in C is that in C, just the value of variables get passed to the subroutine, not the variables themselves. QuickBasic defaults to passing the actual variables, which are then modified while they're in the subroutine. This makes it necessary for us to save the variables before we enter the subroutine, and restore them on returning.

continued from previous page

```
            x = x1
            y = y1

            x = x + height * COS(theta * rad)
            y = y + height * SIN(theta * rad)

            x2 = x
            y2 = y

            level = level - 1

            LINE (x1, y1)-(x2, y2), 15
            PRINT #1, USING " + object {cone ⇐
<###.###,###.###,###.###>,###.###,<###.###,###.###,###.###>,###.### ⇐
matte__white }"; x1, y1, 0, height * scale / twig, x2, y2, 0, height * scale ⇐
* scale / twig

        IF (level > 0) THEN
            ' left-hand sides
                theta = Ang(x1, y1, x2, y2)
                theta = theta + angle
                levelsave = level
                CALL Branch(x2, y2, scale * height, level)
                level = levelsave

            ' right-hand sides
                theta = Ang(x1, y1, x2, y2)
                theta = theta - angle
                levelsave = level
                CALL Branch(x2, y2, scale * height, level)
                level = levelsave
    END IF
END SUB
```

How It Works

The program draws the initial trunk, then calls a function that determines the angle of that segent with respect to the *x* axis. It adds *angle* to it, and goes to a subroutine that generates a branch at that angle, but not before it saves the current level:

```
theta = Ang(x1, y1, x2, y2)
theta = theta + angle
levelsave = level
CALL Branch(x2, y2, scale * height, level)
level = levelsave
```

The *Branch* subroutine calculates a vector at the appropriate angle and length and adds it to the current top of the tree. It decrements the level and, if it's not at the last level, it calls itself. All the left-hand branch sides are completed first. It then goes back and completes the right hand sides, starting at the tips and working its way back to the trunk.

We index the scale so that the fan grows a little bit longer each frame. We also index the diameter of the branches so the tree gets thicker as it grows downward. We use cones rather than cylinders to define the branches, so that as the twigs get smaller and smaller, they still match at the junctions.

A short Polyray data file uses this information to visualize our tree.

```
include "\ply\colors.inc"

viewpoint {
    from <0,75,-125>
    at <0,32.5,0>
    up <0,1,0>
    angle 30
    resolution 320,200
    aspect 1.433
    }
background SkyBlue

object {disk <0,0,0>, <0,1,0>, 1500 matte_blue}

spot_light <2,1,.5>, <0,500,-500>,<0,0,0>,3,5,20

include "anim.inc"
```

The animation uses external include files containing 511 cones each, numbered from FAN01.INC to FAN27.INC. We use the normal animation batch file that writes the desired include file for that frame and calls Polyray, giving it sequential output files to write to.

```
echo include "c:\qb\fan01.inc" > anim.inc
\ply\polyray fan.pi -o fan01.tga
echo include "c:\qb\fan02.inc" > anim.inc
\ply\polyray fan.pi -o fan02.tga
...
```

The output grows from a slender form to a flat fan that fills the screen. Frame 15 is shown in Figure 8-2.

8.2 How do I...
Generate recursively layered objects?

You'll find the code for this in: PLY\CHAPTER8\ITERBOX

Problem

Objects comprised of thousands of individual pieces can be tedious to design. Layered recursion, where a single object definition is called several times from within another definition, which in turn gets called several times from within yet another definition, allows construction of incredibly detailed objects with only a very small amount of code.

Technique

Eric Deren created a recursive object in POV-Ray that kicked off all sorts of other iterative animations. The trick here is to define an object, call it several times from within another object, call the resulting object several times from within a third object, and so on. Pretty soon, no more free memory. Then you reboot.

Steps

The following program (RECBOX.BAS) generates Eric's iterative box without using a ray tracer. It uses some hard-coded box drawing code that runs very fast:

```
'========================================================================
'   RECBOX - Recursive Box -
'
'   Reads a unit cell, and does a  hard-coded turtle graphics
'   double paint deal to show it in fake 3D.  Habit forming.
'   Use only as directed.

DECLARE SUB boxer (m, n, o, k)
SCREEN 12
DIM red(16), green(16), blue(16)
FOR y = 1 TO 4
        FOR x = 1 TO 4
                colornum = x + ((y - 1) * 4) - 1
                READ red(colornum), green(colornum), blue(colornum)
                KOLOR = 65536 * blue(colornum) + 256 * green(colornum) +
red(colornum)
                PALETTE colornum, KOLOR
                COLOR colornum
        NEXT x
NEXT y


'rainbow palette

DATA  0,  0,  0
DATA 16, 16, 16
DATA 32, 32,  32
DATA 0, 0,  0
DATA 63, 32,  0
DATA 58, 56,  0
DATA 16, 42,  0
DATA  0, 30, 36
```

```
DATA  0, 20, 40
DATA  0, 10, 48
DATA  0,  0, 63
DATA 20,  0, 53
DATA 23,  0, 29
DATA 19,  7, 17
DATA 50, 40, 45
DATA 63, 63, 63

WINDOW (-32, -16)-(32, 32) 'a,b,c
'WINDOW (-96, -48)-(96, 96) ' a,b,c,d
units = 3
pi = 3.14159

n = 1
m = 20
FOR z = 1 TO units
  FOR y = 1 TO units
        FOR x = 1 TO units
                READ state(x, y, z)
                n = n + 1
        NEXT x
  NEXT y
NEXT z

LOCATE 4, 68: PRINT "Unit Cell"

' Pick your unit cell here
' the long way - 0 = empty, the color of anything else is set by a cube
' number - anything over 8 or 12 is white
' iteration makes 'em add

DATA 1,1,1
DATA 1,0,1
DATA 1,1,1

DATA 1,0,1
DATA 0,0,0
DATA 1,0,1

DATA 1,1,1
DATA 1,0,1
DATA 1,1,1

' show the patterns
y1 = -5
y2 = 5
y3 = 15
x1 = 20
scale = 2
FOR x = 1 TO units
  FOR y = 1 TO units
```

continued on next page

continued from previous page

```
LINE (.547667 + x, -.370891 + y)-(1.384184 + x, -.146747 + y), 3
LINE (1.384184 + x, -.146747 + y)-(1.401521 + x, .754474 + y), 3
LINE (1.401521 + x, .754474 + y)-(.565005 + x, .53033 + y), 3
LINE (.565005 + x, .53033 + y)-(.547667 + x, -.370891 + y), 3
PAINT (.974594 + x, .191791 + y), 2 + k, 3
LINE (.853854 + x, 1.125365 + y)-(1.401521 + x, .754474 + y), 3
LINE (.017337 + x, .901221 + y)-(.565005 + x, .53033 + y), 3
LINE (.853854 + x, 1.125365 + y)-(.017337 + x, .901221 + y), 3
PAINT (.618151 + x, .889663 + y), 4 + k, 3
LINE (.017337 + x, .901221 + y)-(x, y), 3
LINE (x, y)-(.547667 + x, -.370891 + y), 3
PAINT (.141251 + x, .265165 + y), 6 + k, 3
```

END SUB

When you run the code, you end up with a box like the one shown in Figure 8-3.

We've listed this simulation code because it illustrates how nested loops can generate more and more detail. The last layer has been commented out, but provided you had enough screen resolution and memory, you could carry the recursive process on indefinitely.

Now let's switch to the Polyray file ITERATE.PI. This object is an interesting three-level recursive cube. The camera bobs up and down as it rotates on a spinning platform, giving a good sense of the spacial orientation in the interior of the box:

Figure 8-3 Menger sponge iterative cubical box

```
// ITERATE.PI
// Iterative Box Generator

start_frame 0
end_frame 89
total_frames 90

outfile "iter"

define pi 3.1415927
define rad pi/180

define vy 22.5 + 22.5*cos((frame+12)*4*rad)

// set up the camera
viewpoint {
   from <75,vy,-65>
   at <0,-5,0>
   up <0,1,0>
   angle 45
   hither 1
   aspect 1.433
   resolution 320,200
   }

// get various surface finishes
background MidnightBlue
light <1, 1, 1>, < 60, 50, -50>
light <0.75, 0.75, 0.75>, < 0, 50, -15>
light <1, 1, 1>, < 0, 0, 0>

define Purple <0.714,0.427,0.639>
define BluGre <0.075,0.760,0.64 >

define BozoFunk
texture {
   noise surface {
      color white
      position_fn 1
      lookup_fn 1
      octaves 7
      turbulence 3
      ambient 0.2
      diffuse 0.6
      specular 0.3
      microfacet Reitz 5
      color_map(
        [0.00, 0.35, BluGre, 0.000, BluGre, 0.000 ]
        [0.35, 0.40, BluGre, 0.000, Purple, 0.000 ]
        [0.40, 0.65, Purple, 0.000, Purple, 0.000 ]
        [0.65, 0.90, Purple, 0.000, BluGre, 0.000 ]
```

continued on next page

the number of individual items simply grows too large. But looking at the box, we're really only dealing with a tiny part that's visible—the outside. If we can cut away the parts that don't show, maybe we can get the item count down to where it doesn't exceed the system's capacity.

Warning

A word of caution: if you get the message "Failed to allocate CSG node" or "Cannot allocate transformation," you're going to have to either get more memory or make a simpler model. This animation will not run in 16MB RAM—you need 32MB.

Technique

An interesting result of cutting away details is that it's an iterative process too. Four levels are shown in the following Polyray code, and // comment lines delete the parts we don't need. We use the tumbling code of Section 2.6, here in its simplest form, to orbit the iterative box and show the details of its construction.

Steps

There are two steps that extend the previous section's code to this one.

1. Copy the third layer, paste it below the previous code, and edit references to *cheese2* to read *cheese3*. This builds the next layer.
2. Go through the code and remove all those items that are not visible from the camera's vantage point.

This step requires looking at a sketch of the cube and, taking each of the 27 members of a layer, determining which ones won't be visible from that perspective. All we need to do is keep the elements for the three sides facing the camera, which without duplication amounts to the nine top members, the six lower members on one side, and four members on the other, for a total of 19. Since each side is already missing its middle member, that drops the count to 16. Here is the code for this (ITER*.PI).

```
//ITER*.PI
// Iterative Box Deal

start_frame 0
end_frame 359
total_frames 360

define index 360/total_frames
```

```
outfile "iter"

define pi 3.14159
define rad pi/180


define ang1 (frame*index + 0) * rad
define ang2 (frame*index + 60) * rad
define ang3 (frame*index + 120) * rad

define vx 300*SIN(ang1)
define vy 300*SIN(ang2)
define vz 300*SIN(ang3)

// set up the camera
viewpoint {
   from <vx,vy,vz>
   at <0,-30,0>
   up <0,1,0>
   angle 40
   hither 1
   aspect 1.433
   resolution 320,200
   }

// get various surface finishes
background MidnightBlue
light <1, 1, 1>, < 180, 150, -150>
light <0.75, 0.75, 0.75>, < 0, 100, -15>
light <1, 1, 1>, < 0, 0, 0>

// set up background color & lights
include "\PLY\COLORS.INC"

// define a short pyramid made out of progressively smaller boxes
define cheese
object {
    object { box <-3, -3, -3>, <3, 3, 3> }
  - object { box <-3.01, -1, -1>, <3.01, 1, 1>}
  - object { box <-1, -3.01, -1>, <1, 3.01, 1>}
  - object { box <-1, -1, -3.01>, <1, 1, 3.01>}
    }

define cheese2
object {
    object { cheese translate <-6,-6, -6> }
  + object { cheese translate < 0,-6, -6> }
  + object { cheese translate < 6,-6, -6> }

  + object { cheese translate <-6, 0, -6> }
//// object { cheese translate < 0, 0, -6> }
  + object { cheese translate < 6, 0, -6> }
```

continued on next page

continued from previous page

```
   + object { cheese translate <-6, 6, -6> }
   + object { cheese translate < 0, 6, -6> }
   + object { cheese translate < 6, 6, -6> }


// + object { cheese translate <-6,-6, 0> }
//// object { cheese translate < 0,-6, 0> }
   + object { cheese translate < 6,-6, 0> }
//
//// object { cheese translate <-6, 0, 0> }
//// object { cheese translate < 0, 0, 0> }
//// object { cheese translate < 6, 0, 0> }
//
   + object { cheese translate <-6, 6, 0> }
//// object { cheese translate < 0, 6, 0> }
   + object { cheese translate < 6, 6, 0> }
//
//
// + object { cheese translate <-6,-6, 6> }
// + object { cheese translate < 0,-6, 6> }
   + object { cheese translate < 6,-6, 6> }

// + object { cheese translate <-6, 0, 6> }
//// object { cheese translate < 0, 0, 6> }
   + object { cheese translate < 6, 0, 6> }

   + object { cheese translate <-6, 6, 6> }
   + object { cheese translate < 0, 6, 6> }
   + object { cheese translate < 6, 6, 6> }
}

define cheese3
object {
     object { cheese2 translate <-18,-18, -18> }
   + object { cheese2 translate < 0,-18, -18> }
   + object { cheese2 translate < 18,-18, -18> }

   + object { cheese2 translate <-18, 0, -18> }
//// object { cheese2 translate < 0, 0, -18> }
   + object { cheese2 translate < 18, 0, -18> }

   + object { cheese2 translate <-18, 18, -18> }
   + object { cheese2 translate < 0, 18, -18> }
   + object { cheese2 translate < 18, 18, -18> }


// + object { cheese2 translate <-18,-18, 0> }
//// object { cheese2 translate < 0,-18, 0> }
   + object { cheese2 translate < 18,-18, 0> }
//
//// object { cheese2 translate <-18, 0, 0> }
//// object { cheese2 translate < 0, 0, 0> }
```

```
////  object { cheese2 translate < 18, 0, 0> }
//
    + object { cheese2 translate <-18, 18, 0> }
////  object { cheese2 translate < 0, 18, 0> }
    + object { cheese2 translate < 18, 18, 0> }
//
//
// + object { cheese2 translate <-18,-18, 18> }
// + object { cheese2 translate < 0,-18, 18> }
    + object { cheese2 translate < 18,-18, 18> }

// + object { cheese2 translate <-18, 0, 18> }
////  object { cheese2 translate < 0, 0, 18> }
    + object { cheese2 translate < 18, 0, 18> }

    + object { cheese2 translate <-18, 18, 18> }
    + object { cheese2 translate < 0, 18, 18> }
    + object { cheese2 translate < 18, 18, 18> }
}

define cheese4
object {
      object { cheese3 translate <-54,-54, -54> }
    + object { cheese3 translate < 0,-54, -54> }
    + object { cheese3 translate < 54,-54, -54> }

    + object { cheese3 translate <-54, 0, -54> }
//    object { cheese3 translate < 0, 0, -54> }
    + object { cheese3 translate < 54, 0, -54> }

    + object { cheese3 translate <-54, 54, -54> }
    + object { cheese3 translate < 0, 54, -54> }
    + object { cheese3 translate < 54, 54, -54> }


// + object { cheese3 translate <-54,-54,  0> }
////  object { cheese3 translate < 0,-54,  0> }
    + object { cheese3 translate < 54,-54,  0> }
//
////  object { cheese3 translate <-54, 0,  0> }
////  object { cheese3 translate < 0, 0,  0> }
////  object { cheese3 translate < 54, 0,  0> }
//
    + object { cheese3 translate <-54, 54,  0> }
////  object { cheese3 translate < 0, 54,  0> }
    + object { cheese3 translate < 54, 54,  0> }
//
//
//    object { cheese3 translate <-54,-54,  54> }
// + object { cheese3 translate < 0,-54,  54> }
    + object { cheese3 translate < 54,-54,  54> }
```

continued on next page

```
texture {
   surface {
      ambient Gold, 0.2
      diffuse Gold, 0.8
      specular white, 0.6
      microfacet Phong 5
      reflection white, 0.25
      transmission white, 0, 0
      }
   }
rotate <0.0, -1.0,0.0>
}
```

How It Works

Each level of metaballs in this blob has slightly different strength values, making each level a bit easier to spot as the animation develops. During the course of the animation, various groups of metaballs gang up and protrude from the surface, then dive back in and get lost in the shuffle. The rotational code is included in the BUTTER.BAS as a parameter that is handled every frame. A sample frame from the animation is shown in Figure 8-7.

Differentiating the Image

In BUTTER2.BAS, the entire blob is a single color. It would be more interesting if each level had its own color. The following code produces the data file for this:

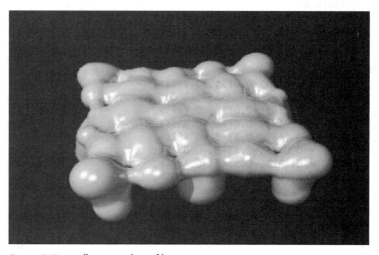

Figure 8-7 A really possessed pat of butter

```
'BUTTER2.BAS
DECLARE SUB rotate (a, b, c)
DECLARE SUB branch (a, b, c, d)

TYPE vector
  a AS SINGLE
  b AS SINGLE
  c AS SINGLE
  d AS SINGLE
END TYPE

DIM br(1024) AS vector
COMMON SHARED br() AS vector, angle, rad, n, depth, rot, dir

SCREEN 12
WINDOW (-1.6, -1.2)-(1.6, 1.2)

pi = 3.1415927#
rad = pi / 180
dir = 1

FOR rot = 0 TO 89
        height = -.35 + .1 * SIN((4 * rot + 60) * rad)
  count$ = RIGHT$("000" + LTRIM$(STR$(rot)), 3)
  filename$ = "blobr" + count$ + ".pi"
  OPEN filename$ FOR OUTPUT AS #1
PRINT #1, "viewpoint {"
PRINT #1, "   from <1.5,2.0,-2.5>"
PRINT #1, USING "   at <0,##.####,0>"; height
PRINT #1, "   up <0,1,0>"
PRINT #1, "   angle 30"
PRINT #1, "   resolution 320,200"
PRINT #1, "   aspect 1.433"
PRINT #1, "   }"
PRINT #1, ""
PRINT #1, "background MidnightBlue"
PRINT #1, "light white, <-15,30,-25>"
PRINT #1, "light white, < 15,30,-25>"
PRINT #1, ""
PRINT #1, "object {"
PRINT #1, "   blob 0.10:"

angle = 90

n = 1
br(n).a = -1
br(n).b = 0
br(n).c = 1
br(n).d = 0
s = 1
dir = 1
CLS
```

continued on next page

continued from previous page

```
FOR depth = 1 TO 3
        'dir = 1
        LOCATE 1, 1: PRINT "frame="; rot
        olds = n
        FOR z = s TO n
                CALL branch(br(z).a, br(z).b, br(z).c, br(z).d)
                dir = -dir
        NEXT z
        s = olds + 1
   'DO WHILE INKEY$ = "": LOOP
NEXT depth
PRINT #1, USING "   ##.####, ##.###, <##.####,##.####,##.####>"; r, .225, ⇐
br(n).c, -depth / 10, br(n).d
PRINT #1, "    u_steps 20"
PRINT #1, "    v_steps 20"
PRINT #1, "    texture {"
PRINT #1, "        surface {"
PRINT #1, "            ambient Coral, 0.2"
PRINT #1, "            diffuse Coral, 0.8"
PRINT #1, "            specular white, 0.6"
PRINT #1, "            microfacet Phong 5"
PRINT #1, "            reflection white, 0.25"
PRINT #1, "            transmission white, 0, 0"
PRINT #1, "            }"
PRINT #1, "        }"
PRINT #1, USING "    rotate <0.0, ####.#,0.0>"; -rot + 45 * SIN(rot * 4 * rad)
PRINT #1, "    }"
PRINT #1,

n = 1
s = 1
dir = 1
depth = 1

PRINT #1, "object {"
PRINT #1, "    blob 0.09:"


        LOCATE 1, 1: PRINT "frame="; rot
        olds = n
        FOR z = s TO n
                CALL branch(br(z).a, br(z).b, br(z).c, br(z).d)
                dir = -dir
        NEXT z
        s = olds + 1

PRINT #1, USING "   ##.####, ##.###, <##.####,##.####,##.####>"; r, .225, ⇐
br(n).c, -depth / 10, br(n).d
PRINT #1, "    u_steps 20"
PRINT #1, "    v_steps 20"
PRINT #1, "    texture {"
PRINT #1, "        surface {"
PRINT #1, "            ambient Maroon, 0.2"
```

```
PRINT #1, "          diffuse Maroon, 0.8"
PRINT #1, "          specular white, 0.6"
PRINT #1, "          microfacet Phong 5"
PRINT #1, "          reflection white, 0.25"
PRINT #1, "          transmission white, 0, 0"
PRINT #1, "          }"
PRINT #1, "       }"
PRINT #1, USING "   rotate <0.0, ####.#,0.0>"; -rot + 45 * SIN(rot * 4 * rad)
PRINT #1, "    }"
PRINT #1,

depth = 2

PRINT #1, "object {"
PRINT #1, "   blob 0.09:"

          LOCATE 1, 1: PRINT "frame="; rot
          olds = n
          FOR z = s TO n
                  CALL branch(br(z).a, br(z).b, br(z).c, br(z).d)
                  dir = -dir
          NEXT z
          s = olds + 1

PRINT #1, USING "   ##.####, ##.###, <##.####,##.####,##.####>"; r, .225, ⇐
br(n).c, -depth / 10, br(n).d
PRINT #1, "   u_steps 20"
PRINT #1, "   v_steps 20"
PRINT #1, "   texture {"
PRINT #1, "      surface {"
PRINT #1, "          ambient DarkSlateBlue, 0.2"
PRINT #1, "          diffuse DarkSlateBlue, 0.8"
PRINT #1, "          specular white, 0.6"
PRINT #1, "          microfacet Phong 5"
PRINT #1, "          reflection white, 0.25"
PRINT #1, "          transmission white, 0, 0"
PRINT #1, "          }"
PRINT #1, "       }"
PRINT #1, USING "   rotate <0.0, ####.#,0.0>"; -rot + 45 * SIN(rot * 4 * rad)
PRINT #1, "    }"
PRINT #1,

depth = 3

PRINT #1, "object {"
PRINT #1, "   blob 0.09:"

          LOCATE 1, 1: PRINT "frame="; rot
          olds = n
          FOR z = s TO n
                  CALL branch(br(z).a, br(z).b, br(z).c, br(z).d)
                  dir = -dir
          NEXT z
```

continued on next page

continued from previous page

```
            s = olds + 1

PRINT #1, USING "    ##.####, ##.###, <##.####,##.####,##.####>"; r, .225, ⇐
br(n).c, -depth / 10, br(n).d
PRINT #1, "    u_steps 20"
PRINT #1, "    v_steps 20"
PRINT #1, "    texture {"
PRINT #1, "        surface {"
PRINT #1, "            ambient SteelBlue, 0.2"
PRINT #1, "            diffuse SteelBlue, 0.8"
PRINT #1, "            specular white, 0.6"
PRINT #1, "            microfacet Phong 5"
PRINT #1, "            reflection white, 0.25"
PRINT #1, "            transmission white, 0, 0"
PRINT #1, "            }"
PRINT #1, "        }"
PRINT #1, USING "    rotate <0.0, ####.#,0.0>"; -rot + 45 * SIN(rot * 4 * rad)
PRINT #1, "    }"
PRINT #1,

CLOSE #1
NEXT rot

OPEN "doit.bat" FOR OUTPUT AS #2
FOR rot = 0 TO 89
   count$ = RIGHT$("000" + LTRIM$(STR$(rot)), 3)
   PRINT #2, "call pr blobr" + count$
NEXT rot
CLOSE #2

SUB branch (a, b, c, d)

        centerx = (a + c) / 2
        centery = (b + d) / 2
        length = .95 ^ depth * ((a - c) ^ 2 + (b - d) ^ 2) ^ .5

        x = (a - c) + .000001
        y = b - d
        t = ATN(y / x) / rad
        IF x < 0 THEN t = t + 180
        IF t < 0 THEN t = t + 360
        ph = 45

        IF Dir > 0 THEN ph = angle / 2 ELSE ph = 0

        height = -.2 + .15 * SIN((4 * rot + 120 * depth) * rad)

FOR ang = -t + depth * rot * dir TO 360 - angle - t + depth * rot * dir + 1 ⇐
STEP angle
        n = n + 1

        br(n).a = centerx
        br(n).b = centery
```

```
        br(n).c = length * SIN(ang * rad) / 2 + centerx
        br(n).d = length * COS(ang * rad) / 2 + centery

  x1 = br(n).a
  y1 = br(n).b
  z1 = height
  CALL rotate(x1, y1, z1)

  x2 = br(n).c
  y2 = br(n).d
  z2 = height
  CALL rotate(x2, y2, z2)

        LINE (x1, z1)-(x2, z2), depth
        r = length * depth / 8
  x = br(n).c
  y = br(n).d
  z = height
  CALL rotate(x, y, z)
        CIRCLE (x, z), r

        PRINT #1, USING "   ##.####, ##.###, <##.####,##.####,##.####>,"; r, ⇐
.225, br(n).c, height, br(n).d
NEXT ang

END SUB

SUB rotate (x, y, z)

  xrotate = 90
  yrotate = 0
  zrotate = 0

        x0 = x
        y0 = y
        z0 = z

        x1 = x0
        y1 = y0 * COS(xrotate * rad) - z0 * SIN(xrotate * rad)
        z1 = y0 * SIN(xrotate * rad) + z0 * COS(xrotate * rad)

        x2 = z1 * SIN(yrotate * rad) + x1 * COS(yrotate * rad)
        y2 = y1
        z2 = z1 * COS(yrotate * rad) - x1 * SIN(yrotate * rad)

        x3 = x2 * COS(zrotate * rad) - y2 * SIN(zrotate * rad)
        y3 = x2 * SIN(zrotate * rad) + y2 * COS(zrotate * rad)
        z3 = z2

        x = x3
        y = y3
        z = z3

END SUB
```

This second program produces the following Polyray code:

```
viewpoint {
   from <1.5,2.0,-2.5>
   at <0,-0.2601,0>
   up <0,1,0>
   angle 30
   resolution 320,200
   aspect 1.433
   }

background MidnightBlue
light white, <-15,30,-25>
light white, < 15,30,-25>

// main blob

object {
   blob 0.10:
   0.2375,   0.225, <-0.0166,-0.0756,-0.9499>,
   0.2375,   0.225, <-0.9499,-0.0756, 0.0166>,
   0.2375,   0.225, < 0.0166,-0.0756, 0.9499>,
   0.2375,   0.225, < 0.9499,-0.0756,-0.0166>,
   0.2143,   0.225, <-0.4369,-0.3348,-0.4824>,
   ...

   0.1378,   0.225, < 0.8717,-0.1895,-0.0387>,
   0.0000,   0.225, < 0.8717,-0.4000,-0.0387>
   u_steps 20
   v_steps 20
   texture {
      surface {
         ambient Coral, 0.2
         diffuse Coral, 0.8
         specular white, 0.6
         microfacet Phong 5
         reflection white, 0.25
         transmission white, 0, 0
         }
      }
   rotate <0.0,     2.1,0.0>
   }

object {
   blob 0.09:
   0.2375,   0.225, <-0.0166,-0.0756,-0.9499>,
   0.2375,   0.225, <-0.9499,-0.0756, 0.0166>,
   0.2375,   0.225, < 0.0166,-0.0756, 0.9499>,
   0.2375,   0.225, < 0.9499,-0.0756,-0.0166>,
   0.0000,   0.225, < 0.9499,-0.1000,-0.0166>
   u_steps 20
   v_steps 20
   texture {
```

```
      surface {
          ambient Maroon, 0.2
          diffuse Maroon, 0.8
          specular white, 0.6
          microfacet Phong 5
          reflection white, 0.25
          transmission white, 0, 0
          }
      }
   rotate <0.0,    2.1,0.0>
   }

object {
   blob 0.09:
   0.2143,   0.225, <-0.4369,-0.3348,-0.4824>,
   0.2143,   0.225, <-0.0158,-0.3348,-0.0463>,
   0.2143,   0.225, < 0.4203,-0.3348,-0.4674>,
   0.2143,   0.225, <-0.0008,-0.3348,-0.9035>,
   0.2143,   0.225, <-0.4525,-0.3348, 0.4364>,
   0.2143,   0.225, <-0.0468,-0.3348,-0.0141>,
   0.2143,   0.225, <-0.4974,-0.3348,-0.4198>,
   0.2143,   0.225, <-0.9030,-0.3348, 0.0307>,
   0.2143,   0.225, < 0.4369,-0.3348, 0.4824>,
   0.2143,   0.225, < 0.0158,-0.3348, 0.0463>,
   0.2143,   0.225, <-0.4203,-0.3348, 0.4674>,
   0.2143,   0.225, < 0.0008,-0.3348, 0.9035>,
   0.2143,   0.225, < 0.4525,-0.3348,-0.4364>,
   0.2143,   0.225, < 0.0468,-0.3348, 0.0141>,
   0.2143,   0.225, < 0.4974,-0.3348, 0.4198>,
   0.2143,   0.225, < 0.9030,-0.3348,-0.0307>,
   0.0000,   0.225, < 0.9030,-0.2000,-0.0307>
   u_steps 20
   v_steps 20
   texture {
      surface {
          ambient DarkSlateBlue, 0.2
          diffuse DarkSlateBlue, 0.8
          specular white, 0.6
          microfacet Phong 5
          reflection white, 0.25
          transmission white, 0, 0
          }
      }
   rotate <0.0,    2.1,0.0>
   }

object {
   blob 0.09:
   0.1378,   0.225, <-0.2354,-0.1895,-0.2953>,
   0.1378,   0.225, <-0.0393,-0.1895,-0.4658>,
   ...
   ...
   0.1378,   0.225, < 0.6698,-0.1895,-0.2023>,
```

continued on next page

441

continued from previous page

```
    0.1378,  0.225, < 0.5062,-0.1895,-0.0003>,
    0.1378,  0.225, < 0.7082,-0.1895, 0.1633>,
    0.1378,  0.225, < 0.8717,-0.1895,-0.0387>,
    0.0000,  0.225, < 0.8717,-0.3000,-0.0387>
  u_steps 20
  v_steps 20
  texture {
    surface {
        ambient SteelBlue, 0.2
        diffuse SteelBlue, 0.8
        specular white, 0.6
        microfacet Phong 5
        reflection white, 0.25
        transmission white, 0, 0
        }
    }
rotate <0.0,    2.1,0.0>
}
```

This code includes not only the object from our first animation, but each level separately declared as individual blobs, now colored Maroon, DarkSlateBlue and SteelBlue. The three levels of this blob are slightly different sizes, and they peek out from around one another at various times (Figure 8-8).

Batch Run

The only other thing that's needed is a batch file to call each data file sequentially. That is automatically generated by the QuickBasic code as a file called DOIT.BAT.

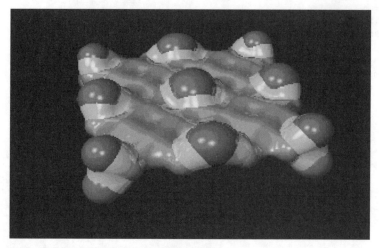

Figure 8-8 Four cavorting nested multicolored blobs

```
call pr blobr000
call pr blobr001
call pr blobr002
call pr blobr003
call pr blobr004
call pr blobr005
call pr blobr006
call pr blobr007
call pr blobr008
call pr blobr009
call pr blobr010
call pr blobr011
call pr blobr012
call pr blobr013
...
```

 ## 8.5 How do I...
Make a pentagonal kaleidoscope?

You'll find the code for this in: PLY\CHAPTER8\KALE1

Problem

Kaleidoscopes are usually done with bits of colored glass and a triangular mirrored tunnel, which form a regularly repeating pattern that goes out in all directions. We can use recursion to make our kaleidoscope out of real objects, allowing us to create symmetries that aren't possible with mirrors. Mirrors will be used for creating extended reflections, not for generating symmetry.

Technique

We'll generate a header file for the static elements, then write a short QuickBasic program to define four successive layers of recursive elements. While you may not believe this, the entire recursive array (37 pages of code) was originally written using nothing more than macros in an editor and a series of block copies. You're being spared this task by our resorting to some simple loops in QuickBasic.

Steps

KALE1.PI, the Polyray header file for this, is standard:

continued from previous page

```
FOR c = 1 TO 5
FOR d = 1 TO 5
v1$ = "L" + CHR$(48 + a) + CHR$(48 + b) + CHR$(48 + c) + CHR$(48 + d)
IF b > 0 THEN n = 3
IF a > 0 THEN n = 4
PRINT #1, "object { sphere "; v1$; ", "; t$(n); " }"
NEXT d
PRINT #1,
NEXT c
PRINT #1,
NEXT b
PRINT #1,
NEXT a
CLOSE #1
```

This code creates two basic blocks of data. The first defines time variable positions for the elements:

```
define L0001   rotate(<1,0,0>,<0,0,br+360*1/5>)
define L0002   rotate(<1,0,0>,<0,0,br+360*2/5>)
define L0003   rotate(<1,0,0>,<0,0,br+360*3/5>)
define L0004   rotate(<1,0,0>,<0,0,br+360*4/5>)
define L0005   rotate(<1,0,0>,<0,0,br+360*5/5>)

define L0011 rotate((L0001*0.5 + <0.5,0,-0.25>),<0,0,br+360*1/5>)
define L0012 rotate((L0001*0.5 + <0.5,0,-0.25>),<0,0,br+360*2/5>)
define L0013 rotate((L0001*0.5 + <0.5,0,-0.25>),<0,0,br+360*3/5>)
define L0014 rotate((L0001*0.5 + <0.5,0,-0.25>),<0,0,br+360*4/5>)
define L0015 rotate((L0001*0.5 + <0.5,0,-0.25>),<0,0,br+360*5/5>)

define L0021 rotate((L0002*0.5 + <0.5,0,-0.25>),<0,0,br+360*1/5>)
define L0022 rotate((L0002*0.5 + <0.5,0,-0.25>),<0,0,br+360*2/5>)
define L0023 rotate((L0002*0.5 + <0.5,0,-0.25>),<0,0,br+360*3/5>)
define L0024 rotate((L0002*0.5 + <0.5,0,-0.25>),<0,0,br+360*4/5>)
define L0025 rotate((L0002*0.5 + <0.5,0,-0.25>),<0,0,br+360*5/5>)
```

...

The second block places spheres at the positions specified by these vectors:

```
object { sphere L0001, 0.12 reflective_lightsteelblue }
object { sphere L0002, 0.12 reflective_lightsteelblue }
object { sphere L0003, 0.12 reflective_lightsteelblue }
object { sphere L0004, 0.12 reflective_lightsteelblue }
object { sphere L0005, 0.12 reflective_lightsteelblue }

object { sphere L0011, 0.1  reflective_navy }
object { sphere L0012, 0.1  reflective_navy }
object { sphere L0013, 0.1  reflective_navy }
object { sphere L0014, 0.1  reflective_navy }
object { sphere L0015, 0.1  reflective_navy }

object { sphere L0021, 0.1  reflective_navy }
```

```
object { sphere L0022, 0.1  reflective_navy }
object { sphere L0023, 0.1  reflective_navy }
object { sphere L0024, 0.1  reflective_navy }
object { sphere L0025, 0.1  reflective_navy }

...
```

Each recursive layer is given its own color.

How It Works

This animation contains four basic layers of pentagons, each built on the previous layer. Each layer is signified by a nonzero element in its name, as shown in Table 8-1.

Items in level	Name of level	Color
5	L0001-L0005	reflective_lightsteelblue
25	L0011-L0055	reflective_navy
125	L0111-L0555	reflective_yellow
625	L1111-L5555	reflective_coral

Table 8-1 Item count, object names, and colors for the kaleidoscope spheres

We built each layer based on the midpoint of the previous layer plus an offset, and spin each layer so that the entire figure gears in a coordinated fashion. We've placed this entire figure inside a mirrored cone whose tip moves toward and away from the camera. Another mirror behind the camera provides additional reflections inside the cone:

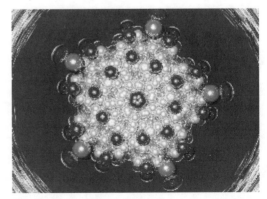

Figure 8-9 Pentagonal kaleidoscope

```
define tip -1.5+sin(radians(frame*5))
light white*0.75, <0,0,tip+0.1>

object { cone <0,0,tip>,0,<0,0,5>,10 mir2 }
object { disc <0,0,5>,<0,0,-1>,10 mir2 }
```

A combination of coordinated movement and shifting reflections makes an amazingly complex animation (see Figure 8-9) that's better than most real kaleidoscopes.

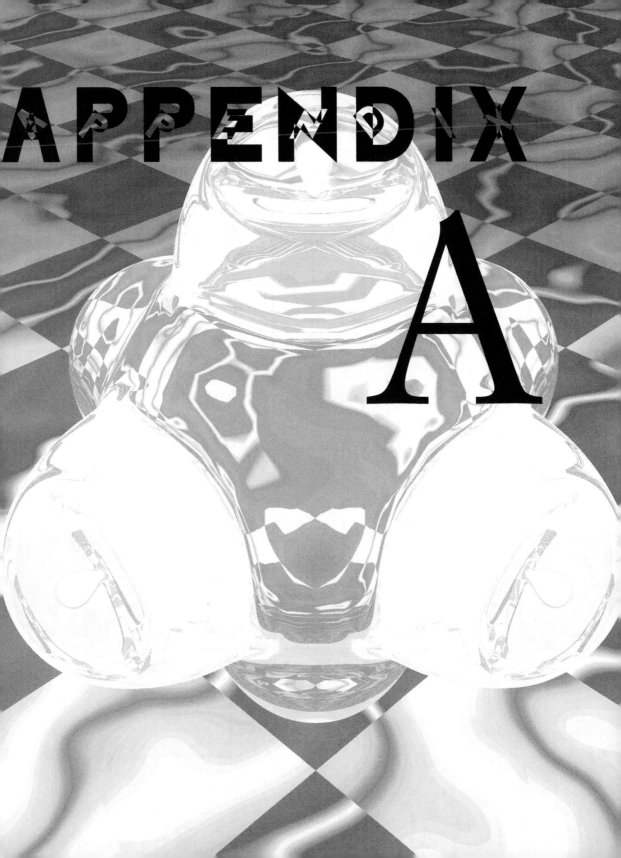

APPENDIX

A

A

TOOLS REFERENCE

Using QuickBasic

Almost every animation created in this book is done with the assistance of QuickBasic. It's great for generating simulations and plotting mathematical functions. It's not particularly powerful or as portable as a language like C, but for what we're using it for, it doesn't have to be. It's easy to write code that runs right the first time.

Loading and Running

Even if you're new to QuickBasic, you'll be able to pick up what's being done here fairly fast. More information on the QBASIC IDE (Integrated Development Environment) can be found in the DOS documentation. The programs have already been written for you; running them is as simple as typing QBASIC (distributed with DOS) or QB, loading a .BAS file and running it. You may choose to use a mouse to move through the menus, or use the short cut commands to accomplish these actions.

The shortcut command for opening a file is (ALT)-(F), then (O), bringing up a menu that displays the files available in the current directory. You can either pick one or change to the directory where the one you want resides. Once the file is loaded, select (R)un (S)tart or use the short-cut command (SHIFT)-(F 5) to run the program. The program finishes, instructs you to press any key to continue, and returns you to the text listing. To toggle back to the output screen, press the (F 4) key. Believe it or not, that just about covers all you really need to know about running QuickBasic code.

Step-by-Step Example

1. Change to the PLY\CHAPTER2\BOLITA directory.
2. Enter either QBASIC or QB depending on which version you have.
3. Select (F)ile (O)pen, and pick COLLIDE.BAS.
4. Select (R)un (S)tart.
5. Watch the animation run. Press (ESC) when bored.
6. Press the spacebar to return to the text listing of the program.
7. Press the (F 4) key twice, once to go back to the output screen, once to return to the text listing.
8. Exit QBASIC or QB by pressing (ALT)-(F), then (X).

That's all there is to running QuickBasic Programs.

Editors

You'll need to develop a basic understanding of the syntax, which for the most part is fairly simple. The best way to learn any programming language is by example. You see something interesting, read the code, and extract those things you find useful. This is where a good text editor, one that allows multiple windows to view several programs at once, and skill using cut and paste command come in very handy. The shareware editor Q or the expensive but wonderful editor BRIEF are two fine examples, but EDIT (which comes with DOS) or even NOTEPAD (which comes with Windows) can suffice if that's all you have.

QuickBasic Program Structure

Most programs start by defining the screen and setting the extents and colors. Then some math is done, put on the screen, and animated. Finally, files are opened to write the information to the disk, most times Polyray data files, which generate the final images and animations. Let's go over how these operations are done.

Setting Graphics Mode

Every program displaying graphics selects a video mode and defines coordinates for the lower left and upper right corners of the screen. We'll use mode 12, which gives us a 640 x 480, 16 color screen, since all VGA's can do it, and it's fairly high resolution. Depending on the size of the objects you plan to use, the WINDOW command sets the appropriate size, but you should always keep a 4 x 3 aspect ratio between x and y, for example (1.6, 1.2), (80,60) and (320,240), otherwise images you simulate will end up being stretched or squashed in the ray tracer. An example of setting up the graphics screen follows:

```
SCREEN 12
WINDOW (-320,-240)-(320,240)
```

The default values for the colors in the VGA palette are not only random, they're unpleasant, and what's worse, there are only 16 of them. Often you'll want to use color to show depth, which only works if the colors are in some logical order, like a rainbow. Achieving a rainbow palette, with colors that progress from red to violet, is accomplished with the following code. The DATA statements hold 16 sets of intensities for red, green, and blue, one set for each palette entry, whose values range from 0 to 63. If you don't like the colors here, you can always change them to any of the 262,144 available colors by simply entering different values for red, green, and blue in the DATA statements.

```
FOR y = 1 TO 4
   FOR x = 1 TO 4
      colornum = x + ((y - 1) * 4) - 1
      READ red(colornum), green(colornum), blue(colornum)
      KOLOR = 65536 * blue(colornum) + 256 * green(colornum) + red(colornum)
      PALETTE colornum, KOLOR
      COLOR colornum
   NEXT x
```

continued on next page

continued from previous page
```
NEXT y


' Rainbow Palette

DATA  0,  0,  0
DATA 32,  0,  0
DATA 42,  0,  0
DATA 58, 16,  0
DATA 63, 32,  0
DATA 58, 56,  0
DATA 16, 42,  0
DATA  0, 30, 36
DATA  0, 20, 40
DATA  0, 10, 48
DATA  0,  0, 63
DATA 20,  0, 53
DATA 23,  0, 29
DATA 19,  7, 17
DATA 50, 40, 45
DATA 63, 63, 63
```

Vectors and Arrays

Math depends on what you plan to do with it, so there's not much in the way of guidelines that can be offered here, other than try to use vectors and arrays whenever possible. QuickBasic allows user defined data structures that come in very handy for holding sets of logically connected variables. Consider the following code:

```
TYPE Vector
   x AS SINGLE
   y AS SINGLE
   z AS SINGLE
END TYPE

DIM penta(5) AS Vector

FOR a = 0 to 360 STEP 72
   x = SIN(a * rad)
   y = COS(a * rad)
   penta(i).x = x
   penta(i).y = y
   penta(i).z = 0
   i = i + 1
NEXT a
```

The preceding code defines a data type called a *Vector* that holds three variables: x, y and z. Rather than using a clumsy two-dimensional array, such as *penta(1,3)*, and then having to keep track of which number refers to the axis and which one refers to the actual point number, *Vector* keeps it clear for us. The variable *penta(3).x* is the third point's *x* value. Arrays must be given room for storage, which is where the DIM statement comes in. The variable *penta* can hold five sets of three values each. If you wanted it to hold 100, you'd have to use

```
DIM penta(100) as Vector
```

Do try to make your variable names meaningful to total strangers, as you'll be one yourself about a week after you've finished writing this code and gone on to bigger and better things.

File I/O

Files are opened by specifying a text name for them and assigning a number to the stream that results. The concept of data flow as streams is picturesque; the normal input stream is the keyboard, the output stream the video monitor. Redirecting that flow to a file is as easy as opening a stream and directing its output there.

The following OPEN statement is broken up into two lines here, for clarity. It could just as easily be done with one line, but then we wouldn't get a chance to mention string variables. Variables with $ signs at the ends are string variables. Strings are a series of characters, as opposed to numeric variables like *x* and *frame,* which are single numbers.

```
file$ = "\test\pinkfloy.d"
OPEN file$ FOR OUTPUT AS #1
x = 1
frame = 2
PRINT #1, x, frame
PRINT #1, "Hello, (hello), ((hello)), is anybody IN there?"
PRINT #1, "Just nod if you can HEAR me."
CLOSE #1
```

This opens a file called PINKFLOY.D in the test directory and subsequent PRINT #1, statements put data not up on the screen, but into this file stream. Running this program would produce the following file, PINKFLOY.D:

```
1       2
Hello, (hello), ((hello)), is anybody IN there?
Just nod if you can HEAR me.
```

Note that QuickBasic will not make the test directory for you if one doesn't already exist, but it's not shy about issuing an error message informing you of this problem. To run this, create a test directory first.

Sequential Numbering

Numbered lists come up so often that they deserve a few minutes of consideration here. Let's say you're trying to generate a sequential list of numbered variables. Variables are strings, and numbers can be converted to strings with the STR$() function. Your first attempt is

```
For x = 1 to 15
   item$= "item"+str$(x)
   print item$
next x
```

The output of this is

```
item 1
item 2
item 3
...
```

The problem with these variables is they all have spaces in them, which isn't allowed. QuickBasic has an LTRIM$() function that removes leading blank characters from strings, so next we try

```
For x = 1 to 15
   item$= "item"+ LTRIM$(str$(x))
   print item$
next x
```

The output of this is

```
item1
item2
item3
...
item9
item10
item11
item12
...
```

The only problem with this is that if you passed these variables to a program that needed to process these items in order, the order it would pick would be

```
item1
item10
item11
...
item2
```

In other words, it puts variable 2 after variables 11-19. This problem can be addressed by using leading zeros—as many as will allow an unambiguous order for the largest number you need to use.

Consider the following loop:

```
OPEN "test" for output as #1
pref$ = "test"
FOR frame = 0 to 15
    frame.count$ = RIGHT$("0000" + LTRIM$(STR$(frame)), 4)
    frame.pi$ = pref$ + frame.count$ + ".pi"
    frame.tga$ = pref$ + frame.count$ + ".tga"
    PRINT #1, frame.pi$
    PRINT #1, frame.tga$
NEXT frame
CLOSE #1
```

This code creates a file called TEST that contains the following text:

```
test0000.pi
test0000.tga
test0001.pi
test0001.tga
test0002.pi
...
test0009.pi
test0009.tga
test0010.pi
test0010.tga
test0011.pi
test0011.tga
...
```

Consider the case where *frame* = 5. The line

```
frame.count$ = RIGHT$("0000" + LTRIM$(STR$(frame)), 4)
```

converts the value for *frame* to a string, tacks it onto the end of the string "0000", to make the five character string "00005". It then trims the result to include only the right four digits. This gives us "0005". You'll find this comes in very handy at times.

PRINT #1, USING...

Another useful construct is the PRINT #1, USING ... command, which allows you to specify the positions and lengths of variables inside PRINT expressions. A five character string expression is located in the PRINT #1, USING statement by including the structure "\   \" (a backslash, three spaces and another backslash) where you want the variable to go, and numeric expressions that specify the number of digits and the placement of the decimal point using "#.###" structures. The following example:

```
v1$ = "L0001"
v2$ = "L0100"
d = 3
```

continued on next page

continued from previous page

```
PRINT #1, USING
"define \    \ rotate((\    \*0.5 + <0.5,0,-0.25>),<0,0,br+360*#/5>)"; v1$, v2$, d
```

writes this line to file #1:

```
define L0001 rotate((L0100*0.5 + <0.5,0,-0.25>),<0,0,br+360*3/5>)
```

Underscores

A common delimiting character in C programs, used liberally in the COLORS.INC file in Polyray, is the underscore character "_". QuickBasic interprets this as a formatting character in PRINT USING statements. The following program

```
OPEN "test" FOR OUTPUT AS #1
var$ = "L0001"
PRINT #1, var$; " shiny_red"
PRINT #1, USING "\    \ shiny_red"; var$
PRINT #1, USING "\    \ shiny__red"; var$
CLOSE #1
```

generates this output:

```
L0001 shiny_red
L0001 shinyred
L0001 shiny_red
```

In a simple PRINT statement, the underscore is passed as just another character. In the first PRINT USING statement, its use changes to mean "print the next character as a literal character." This allows for things like printing # symbols in PRINT USING statements, rather than their being treated as placeholders for numeric variables. In the second line, it prints the literal value for *r*, which is just *r*, and the underscore disappears. The third line uses two underscores, which prints the second underscore as a literal underscore, giving us what we needed.

Quotation Marks

Polyray data files require quotation marks surrounding include files such as "colors.inc".

```
include "colors.inc"
```

PRINT statements use quotation marks to signify the ends of string variables. To get a PRINT statement to generate a quotation mark, you break the strings up and insert the ASCII code for a quotation mark (CHR$(34)) as just another component to be printed. The following print statement

```
PRINT #1, "include "; CHR$(34); "colors.inc"; CHR$(34)
```

writes the line

```
include "colors.inc"
```

to the output file #1.

Using Polyray

Installation

The CD contains an installation program that will automatically load the Polyray program, the data files, and all the utilities required into their proper locations. Let's cover the directory structure that results and what it does for us. The main directory for Polyray is PLY and everything is loaded as subdirectories off this one, resulting in the following organization:

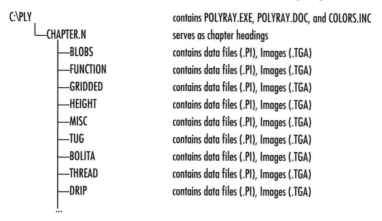

```
C:\PLY                          contains POLYRAY.EXE, POLYRAY.DOC, and COLORS.INC
   └─CHAPTER.N                  serves as chapter headings
       ├─BLOBS                  contains data files (.PI), Images (.TGA)
       ├─FUNCTION               contains data files (.PI), Images (.TGA)
       ├─GRIDDED                contains data files (.PI), Images (.TGA)
       ├─HEIGHT                 contains data files (.PI), Images (.TGA)
       ├─MISC                   contains data files (.PI), Images (.TGA)
       ├─TUG                    contains data files (.PI), Images (.TGA)
       ├─BOLITA                 contains data files (.PI), Images (.TGA)
       ├─THREAD                 contains data files (.PI), Images (.TGA)
       ├─DRIP                   contains data files (.PI), Images (.TGA)
       ...
```

The executable program POLYRAY.EXE and the Polyray documentation file POLYRAY.DOC reside in the main PLY. Any time you need access to the docs, enter:

EDIT \PLY\POLYRAY.DOC

and a full text listing of the documentation file will appear. You might also print out a copy of this, but paper can't be searched for keyword matches as easily as this electronic copy.

The include files for colors and textures commonly used in all images are placed in the PLY directory. The image creation data files, with .PI extentions, reside in subdirectories below that one, collected roughly by topic. The shareware version of Polyray includes a batch file that will create all the sample images supplied with Polyray. We didn't do that with the animations in this book because it would take a long time, and require several gigabytes of disk storage space. TGA files tend to form sprawling mounds, and it's useful, at least from a directory listing standpoint, to herd them together into their own subdirectories, use them to create flics, then blow them away.

Running Polyray

Detailed instructions are found in the Polyray documentation which cover all the intricacies of running Polyray. However, there are a few things you really need to know about it at this stage. We'll go over the basic concepts, give a few shortcuts, and provide a step-by-step example.

Running Polyray involves going to the subdirectory containing the data file you wish to render, entering POLYRAY followed by the name of that file, which has a .PI extension, and (optionally) providing a name for the output image.

POLYRAY *filename* .PI -o *filename* .TGA

This uses the input file *filename* .PI and generates the output image file *filename* .TGA. The default output name is OUT000.TGA, and animations usually specify their own names when they are rendered.

Running Polyray from a Batch File

The preceding example assumed that the program POLYRAY.EXE was somewhere in your PATH. The executable program POLYRAY.EXE is kept in the \PLY directory. Rather than extending your path statement, you can use the batch file PR.BAT, and place that file somewhere in your PATH (like the \DOS or \TOOLS directory if you have one). The PR.BAT batch file reads

\PLY\POLYRAY %1.PI -o %1.TGA %2

Then, when you wanted to render a file called BLOBS.PI, you'd type the line:

PR BLOBS

The first parameter %1 equals BLOBS. This tells POLYRAY to look for the file BLOBS.PI and create an output file called BLOBS.TGA. The %2 parameter is included so that when you want to resume a trace you (or your pet, or the power company) paused, you can enter

PR BLOBS -R

and Polyray will pick up where it left off. If the file BLOBS is not a single image, but rather an animation, the name the batch file suggests (%1, TGA) for the output image will simply be ignored.

Step-by-Step Example

Here's a step-by-step process to follow for all this.

1. Copy the file PR.BAT from the PLY directory to a subdirectory in your path.
2. Type CD \PLY\DAT\BLOBS at the command line.
3. Type PR BLOBS.
4. Wait for the image to finish rendering and display the summary screen.

A file called BLOBS.TGA will have been created on your hard drive. It is a 24-bit targa file that requires some post-processing and image display software to view. We'll cover the next few steps in more detail later on, but to see this image immediately, use the following steps.

5. Enter DTA BLOBS.TGA /fg.
6. Enter AAPLAYHI BLOBS.GIF.

Step 5 converts the 24-bit targa file to an 8-bit .GIF file, which can be viewed using the flic player AAPLAYHI. While it may seem odd to use an animation player to view a static file, hey!, it works. Other programs like CSHOW and VPIC are more commonly used for image viewing, along with several windows programs, but we can't assume you have any of those at this point.

Include Files

The structure we've outlined is important for one other thing. Most Polyray files make use of color and texture definitions found in the files COLORS.INC and TEXTURE.INC. These are included in each Polyray data file (.PI) by the lines:

```
include "\PLY\COLORS.INC"
include "\PLY\TEXTURES.INC"
```

The directory containing these include files must be named "PLY", otherwise references made to them in each datafile would need to be changed.

POLYRAY.INI

The POLYRAY.INI file allows you to specify runtime parameters that control things you probably don't really want to have to worry about every time you run Polyray. While Polyray will run without this file, it defaults to

continued from previous page

```
object {
    sphere <0,0,0>,grow
    shiny_blue
}
```

Creating Image Data Files

You should use whatever tools you're comfortable with to generate your data files. There are now many add-on utilities that allow you to graphically design scenes for your favorite ray tracer (POV Cad, Sculptura, Imagine, RTAG, Animake, MORAY, and many more exist as well) which either output compatible scene source code, or save it in some universally accessible format that can then be translated. Most CAD packages save DXF files, which are gruesome and longwinded but provide a standard format with published specifications, and translators are available to go from this standard to ray tracers.

Sometimes all you need are triangle points $(x1,y1,z1,x2,y2,z2,x3,y3,z3)$ that specify the corners of a bunch of little triangles, which used together define some object, like a cow or Beethoven. It simply becomes a matter of converting this data, one triangle at a time, into acceptable Polyray syntax. This is done using a program, and an example is provided in this book in Section 5.4. Then anything, even objects originally defined for high-end workstations, can be translated into ray tracer compatible data.

Standard paint programs can be used to provide both imagemaps for textures and heightfield data for raised terrains and extruded logos. The ability to import 2-D data to generate 3-D objects is incredibly powerful.

For complicated files containing hundreds or perhaps thousands of items, it is easiest to handle such things programmatically. You first generate a simple file containing a couple of these items, then automate the creation of all the other ones. The ability to use programs to generate image files makes text-based ray tracers much more powerful than graphics-based image creation programs.

Commenting the Data Files

The double backslash (\\), commonly use in C++, is interpreted as "ignore this line, it's just comments." Liberal comments are always a good idea. The only time you'll completely understand your own code is while you're writing it, and later on you'll wonder what possessed you to do something a certain way. Comments rescue you from a continual journey of rediscovery. Comments also come in handy during image development, blocking out unnecessary items to simplify the source code, to make it render faster.

Most code goes through several generations before it looks good enough to keep. Commenting out old code and adding new code gives you an audit trail, allowing you to backtrack to where you were. Also, saving each revision of a file to a sequential name (SURF1.PI, then SURF2.PI, then SURF3.PI...) allows you to keep files around that might not seem important at the time, but provide invaluable clues later on. There's nothing worse than having a really great image, but not having the original data file because later revisions overwrote it.

Internal Versus External Animation Control

Really good animations come about when you motivate static scenes with programs of your own design. Two rough classes of animation are external and internal animation. External animation means you create a series of text files (one per frame) that sequentially generate each image. This is necessary when the data used for the motion is not easily incorporated into Polyray's syntax, or comes from complex programs written in different languages. Internal animation uses a single data file in which variables are controlled by a frame counter that steps the action of static objects through their motion. Internal animation is cleaner in that there are fewer files hanging around. Most of the animations in this book are internal, but examples of external animations are provided as well.

Using DTA

Polyray generates a series of images in a numbered list. For ten frame animation with an outfile specification of HAPPY, it would create the following ten files:

```
HAPPY000.TGA
HAPPY001.TGA
HAPPY002.TGA
HAPPY003.TGA
HAPPY004.TGA
HAPPY005.TGA
HAPPY006.TGA
HAPPY007.TGA
HAPPY008.TGA
HAPPY009.TGA
```

Creating a flic file called HAPPY.FLI from this series might involve entering the following line:

DTA HAPPY*.TGA /oHAPPY /s5

You hand DTA the file prefix for the images, give it an output name HAPPY with /oHAPPY, and tell it to have a playing speed of 5 with /s5. DTA defaults to flic output.

There are many switches in DTA, and please read the documentation for more information on them. They're all very useful, but two in particular are used all the time. If you generate images for your flics that are larger than 320 x 200, you must use the /R6 switch to make a high resolution .FLC from them. There are other modes, so again, read the documentation. A quick summary is also available if you just enter the command DTA by itself with no other parameters.

One of the first tasks DTA must perform is generating an optimal palette to map the 16.7 million possible colors in the TGA files into the best 256 colors to run on a standard VGA or SVGA display. This can be a lengthy process for animations that are several hundred frames long, and if the basic image doesn't change all that much, checking every single TGA file doesn't really make higher quality flic. You can scan, say, every 10th image using the /c10 switch, and this can really cut down the time it takes to make the final flic.

DTA generates GIFs using the /fg switch. As mentioned earlier, the animation player AAPLAYHI can then display these GIFs for you, although VPIC or CSHOW, two popular shareware GIF viewers, are more commonlly used for this task. CSHOW and VPIC can also display TGA files directly.

Step-by-Step Example

Here's a step-by-step process to follow for all this:

1. Change to the the PLY\CHAPTER1\TEST directory.
2. Run the file TESTANIM.PI with Polyray by entering PR TESTANIM.
3. Wait for the ten frames to render.
4. Generate a flic by entering DTA test*.tga /ff /otest /s5.
5. View the flic by entering AAPLAYHI test.fli.
6. Press (ESC) when you're done watching it.

Using AAPLAYHI

AAPLAYHI is a freely distributable animation player program from Autodesk. The default maximum display size is 320 x 200, but with the appropriate video cards and VESA compatible modes, animations as large as 1,024 x 768 can be displayed. It not only works with flics, but will also display GIFs as well.

An AA.CFG file is created every time AAPLAYHI is started from a directory that doesn't contain one, and the screen size may be selected from whatever screen modes AAPLAYHI detects your hardware is capable of.

If your flic is 320 x 200 or smaller, you can run AAPLAYHI directly by entering the command AAPLAYHI *flic*.FLI. Entering AAPLAYHI by itself brings up a graphics screen and identifies the program. You press a mouse key to get to the menus. At this point, you'll either be able to load your flics directly or set the screen size to the appropriate one and load your flics afterwords.

AAPLAYHI will use all your system memory and attempt to load the flic into it, which makes flics play much smoother than directly off your hard drive. While it doesn't mind HIMEM, you cannot have EMM386 providing expanded memory or AAPLAYHI will key on it and miss your extended memory entirely.

Step-by-Step Example

Here's a step-by-step process to follow for all this.

1. Change to the the PLY\CHAPTER1\TEST directory.
2. Enter AAPLAYHI by itself.
3. Press a mouse key to clear the screen.
4. Go to the menu and select Flic, Load, and Test.
5. Press the >> button and watch the flic play.
6. Press any key to pause.
7. Select Program, Quit, and exit AAPLAYHI.

INDEX

ENVIRONMENTAL AWARENESS

Books have a substantial influence on the destruction of the forests of the Earth. For example, it takes 17 trees to produce one ton of paper. A first printing of 30,000 copies of a typical 480 page book consumes 108,000 pounds of paper which will require 918 trees!

Waite Group Press™ is against the clear-cutting of forests and supports reforestation of the Pacific Northwest of the United States and Canada, where most of this paper comes from. As a publisher with several hundred thousand books sold each year, we feel an obligation to give back to the planet. We will therefore support and contribute a percentage of our proceeds to organizations which seek to preserve the forests of planet Earth.

IMAGE LAB

Tim Wegner

This book is a complete PC-based "digital darkroom" that covers virtually all areas of graphic processing and manipulation. It comes with the finest graphics shareware available today: Piclab, CShow, Improces, Image Alchemy, and POV-Ray. This treasure chest of software lets you paint, draw, render and size images, remove colors, adjust palettes, combine, crop, transform, ray trace, and convert from one graphics file to another. Supercharged tutorials show how to make 3-D fractals and combine them to make photorealistic scenes. Plus, all the tools included have support forums on CompuServe so you can easily get the latest help and news.

ISBN 1-878739-11-5, 459 pages, 1-3.5" disk and color poster
$39.95 Available Now

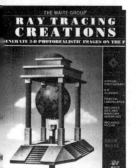

RAY TRACING CREATIONS

Drew Wells and Chris Young

With the *Ray Tracing Creations* book/disk combination, you can immediately begin rendering perfect graphic objects with ease. Using the powerful shareware program POV-Ray, you'll learn to control the location, shape, light, shading, and surface texture of all kinks of 3-D objects. POV-Ray's C-like language is used to describe simple objects, planes, shperes, and more complex polygons. Over 100 incredible pre-built scenes are included that can be generated, studied, and modified in any way you choose. This book provides a complete course in the fundamentals of ray tracing that will challenge and entice you. VGA display required.

ISBN 1-878739-27-1, 600 pages, disk and color plate section
$29.95 Available Now

TO ORDER TOLL FREE CALL 1-800-368-9369
TELEPHONE 415-924-2575 • FAX 415-924-2576
OR SEND ORDER FORM TO: WAITE GROUP PRESS, 200 TAMAL PLAZA, CORTE MADERA, CA 94925

Qty	Book	US/Can Price	Total
____	Flights of Fantasy	$34.95/48.95	____
____	Fractals for Windows	$34.95/48.95	____
____	Image Lab	$39.95/55.95	____
____	Lafore's Windows Programming Made Easy	$29.95/41.95	____
____	Making Movies on Your PC	$34.95/48.95	____
____	Morphing on Your PC	$34.95/48.95	____
____	Multimedia Creations	$44.95/62.95	____
____	Ray Tracing Creations	$39.95/55.95	____
____	Virtual Reality Creations	$34.95/48.95	____
____	Visual Basic How-To, Second Edition	$36.95/51.95	____
____	Visual Basic SuperBible, Second Edition	$39.95/55.95	____
____	Walkthroughs and Flybys CD	$29.95/41.95	____

Calif. residents add 7.25% Sales Tax ____

Shipping

USPS ($5 first book/$1 each add'l) ____
UPS Two Day ($10/$2) ____
Canada ($10/$4) ____

TOTAL ____

Ship to

Name_____

Company _____

Address _____

City, State, Zip_____

Phone _____

ALL ORDERS MUST BE PREPAID

Payment Method
☐ Check Enclosed ☐ VISA ☐ MasterCard

Card#_____ Exp. Date ____

Signature _____

SATISFACTION GUARANTEED
OR YOUR MONEY BACK.

LIMITED WARRANTY

The following warranties shall be effective for 90 days from the date of purchase: (i) The Waite Group, Inc. warrants the enclosed disk to be free of defects in materials and workmanship under normal use; and (ii) The Waite Group, Inc. warrants that the programs, unless modified by the purchaser, will substantially perform the functions described in the documentation provided by The Waite Group, Inc. when operated on the designated hardware and operating system. The Waite Group, Inc. does not warrant that the programs will meet purchaser's requirements or that operation of a program will be uninterrupted or error-free. The program warranty does not cover any program that has been altered or changed in any way by anyone other than The Waite Group, Inc. The Waite Group, Inc. is not responsible for problems caused by changes in the operating characteristics of computer hardware or computer operating systems that are made after the release of the programs, nor for problems in the interaction of the programs with each other or other software.

THESE WARRANTIES ARE EXCLUSIVE AND IN LIEU OF ALL OTHER WARRANTIES OF MERCHANTABILITY OR FITNESS FOR A PARTICULAR PURPOSE OR OF ANY OTHER WARRANTY, WHETHER EXPRESS OR IMPLIED.

EXCLUSIVE REMEDY

The Waite Group, Inc. will replace any defective disk without charge if the defective disk is returned to The Waite Group, Inc. within 90 days from date of purchase.

This is Purchaser's sole and exclusive remedy for any breach of warranty or claim for contract, tort, or damages.

LIMITATION OF LIABILITY

THE WAITE GROUP, INC. AND THE AUTHORS OF THE PROGRAMS SHALL NOT IN ANY CASE BE LIABLE FOR SPECIAL, INCIDENTAL, CONSEQUENTIAL, INDIRECT, OR OTHER SIMILAR DAMAGES ARISING FROM ANY BREACH OF THESE WARRANTIES EVEN IF THE WAITE GROUP, INC. OR ITS AGENT HAS BEEN ADVISED OF THE POSSIBILITY OF SUCH DAMAGES.

THE LIABILITY FOR DAMAGES OF THE WAITE GROUP, INC. AND THE AUTHORS OF THE PROGRAMS UNDER THIS AGREEMENT SHALL IN NO EVENT EXCEED THE PURCHASE PRICE PAID.

COMPLETE AGREEMENT

This Agreement constitutes the complete agreement between The Waite Group, Inc. and the authors of the programs, and you, the purchaser.

Some states do not allow the exclusion or limitation of implied warranties or liability for incidental or consequential damages, so the above exclusions or limitations may not apply to you. This limited warranty gives you specific legal rights; you may have others, which vary from state to state.

SATISFACTION REPORT CARD

Please fill out this card if you want to know of future updates to
Animation How-To CD, or to receive our catalog.

WAITE GROUP PRESS™

Company Name:

Division/Department: Mail Stop:

Last Name: First Name: Middle Initial:

Street Address:

City: State: Zip:

Daytime telephone: (   )

Date product was acquired: Month   Day   Year   Your Occupation:

Overall, how would you rate *Animation How-To CD*?

☐ Excellent   ☐ Very Good   ☐ Good
☐ Fair   ☐ Below Average   ☐ Poor

What did you like MOST about this book?

What did you like LEAST about this book?

**Please describe any problems you may have encountered with
the *Animation How-To CD***

How did you use this book (problem-solver, tutorial, reference...)?

What is your level of computer expertise?

☐ New   ☐ Dabbler   ☐ Hacker
☐ Power User   ☐ Programmer   ☐ Experienced Professional

What computer languages are you familiar with?

Please describe your computer hardware:

Computer _____ Hard disk _____
5.25" disk drives_____ 3.5" disk drives _____
Video card _____ Monitor _____
Printer _____ Peripherals_____
Sound Board_____ CD ROM_____

Where did you buy this book?

☐ Bookstore (name): _____
☐ Discount store (name): _____
☐ Computer store (name): _____
☐ Catalog (name): _____
☐ Direct from WGP   ☐ Other _____

What price did you pay for this book? _____

What influenced your purchase of this book?

☐ Recommendation   ☐ Advertisement
☐ Magazine review   ☐ Store display
☐ Mailing   ☐ Book's format
☐ Reputation of Waite Group Press ☐ Other

How many computer books do you buy each year? _____

How many other Waite Group books do you own? _____

What is your favorite Waite Group book? _____

**Is there any program or subject you would like to see Waite
Group Press cover in a similar approach?** _____

Additional comments? _____

☐ **Check here for a free Waite Group catalog**

Animation How-To CD

Waite Group Press, Inc.

Attention: *Animation How-To CD*

200 Tamal Plaza

Corte Madera, CA 94925

- **FOLD HERE** -